Survival of the Superstitious:
How Religion Helped Ancient Humans Survive

Survival of the Superstitious:
How Religion Helped Ancient Humans Survive

By Genesis Pilgrim

For Kelly,
In memory of our 19th anniversary: November 20th, 2019.
Sending my love from the future.

Table of Contents

How to Use this Book

This book is designed to provide basic catalysts for thought and discussion on human development. As such, you do not need to read this book from cover to cover. Simply find a chapter which suits your fancy. Read a bit, then reflect. If you find yourself reading a chapter which isn't your cup of tea, skip it. Easy peasy.

Although this book is an easy-reader, you will find it will open your understanding to the basic psychological underpinnings which have guided the development of humanity.

My goal is to inspire humans to recognize the contributions of religion to our development. I build a case for a most remarkable position: Religion is at the heart of everything which separates humans from animals. And, in this reality, we find a most paradoxical conclusion . . . When atheism is attempting to pull humanity from religion; religion is the only means through which humanity has flourished for countless generations.

Without religion, human societies do not survive. Thus, within humanity we see *only the superstitious survive*.

And, as we consider the central role religion has played for all our ancient ancestors, we are left to ponder whether or not humanity could even survive if it altogether embraced atheism.

It can't.

As humans lose religion, they directly decrease their chances of survival—especially when confronted with tough times. Religion is the means through which humans have historically survived tragedy and trauma. Religion inspires people with the community, courage and commitment they need to remain true in times of devastation. Atheism does not do this. Therefore, history teaches us atheist human societies are always doomed to collapse—becoming altogether obsolete as they vanish from historical records. When tough times come—as they always do—the faithless humans quickly scatter into obscurity.

If you don't believe me, look at the history of the world. Take note of the ubiquitous presence of religion among *all* ancient human societies. My book will show you "why all ancient human societies were religious."

Whereas Darwin put forth his thoughts on the "survival of the fittest;" within all of human history we see religion is itself the one attribute of humanity which directly determines the possibility for success.

And as a great bane to naturalism and the "survival of the fittest," throughout all of ancient human history we see only the "superstitious survive." Therefore, the religious aspect of humanity is the most significant— directly determining the fitness of a society for long-term survival.

Survival of the Superstitious

Introduction by Genesis Pilgrim

Dear Reader,

Ancient humans were religious—all of them. Why?

Among the myriad of ancient human societies, we would expect to find a large fraction of atheist societies. But we do not. Why?

Instead, our historical records all indicate humanity has always been intertwined with supernatural beliefs. This is profound and points to the fact that our basic identity as humans is connected with spiritual beliefs.

In this book I examine the link between humans and spiritual beliefs. Although I have my own beliefs in the Bible, for the sake of our discussion here I will only be speaking of spirituality *in general*. So, throughout the book, I use the terms "myth," "story," "superstition" and "religion" interchangeably—all to describe spirituality *in general*.

In this book I will contrast between (1) humans with spiritual beliefs and (2) humans with beliefs only in physical things. So, for the sake of discussion, this book will lump together all different spiritual worldviews to compare them to the physical-only atheism worldview.

In this book, I define an "atheist" as a person who believes in nothing supernatural—that is nothing at all beyond the physical. I realize there are atheists, such as some Buddhists who do in fact believe in supernatural things. In this book, I would classify these Buddhists and others like them with the first group of humans with spiritual beliefs.

As you read further you will see why all ancient human societies were religious. Remarkably, I will show you how "spiritual beliefs" cause those with them to be favored for survival. Throughout all of ancient human history, spiritual beliefs have protected individuals and their societies—therefore those ancient people with the strongest beliefs were more likely to survive. Chapter after chapter, I will demonstrate this remarkable fact.

Doubtlessly there were many in history who altogether denied supernatural beliefs in their culture. Yet none of their societies survived effectively in the midst of unrelenting ancient dangers.

In this book, I will clearly explain why all ancient human societies were religious. I will also explain what happened to people in the ancient world who altogether denied the spiritual world.

This will be an entertaining read and I hope you enjoy my analysis of ancient humanity.

Welcome to my book!

Prepare to be enlightened, my friend.

Sincerely,

Genesis Pilgrim

Section I

Humanity's Religious Past

1:

The Religions of Our Ancestors are Better than 21st Century Atheism

As one surveys the different cultures of humanity's past, it becomes apparent they all held supernatural beliefs.

Perhaps the "afterlife" is the most basic spiritual belief. No matter where we look in our past, humans all held ceremony and special significance for their dead. In fact, within physical death itself, a person is ushered into the immediate questioning of the supernatural.

For example, if a dear family member were to pass away in the ancient world, ancient humans would view the physical body of the departed. Although his body was present, the vitality of the man was gone.

So, the question would emerge—how is the man "here," yet he is "not here?"

Immediately, this paradox and the heaviness of grief would move loved ones to think on his vitality, or "soul," continuing to live on—despite the expiration of the man's physical body.

Ultimately, historical records show us all ancient human societies were religious. This is why all ancient humans buried or otherwise honored their dead in special ways.

And, extending from this most basic belief in the afterlife, humans have ever devised many other conceptions of the supernatural—thinking of the many ways in which supernatural power moves into and throughout the physical world. This is a profound thought—yet it bears with it incredible power, allowing humans to shape the world around them by their thoughts alone.

The power inherent within religious thinking demonstrates why humans are inclined toward supernatural beliefs. Within religious beliefs, humans can grant "life" to those who have physically died—comforting their minds with thoughts of how their loved ones continue to "live on."

The ability of humans to think supernaturally is most profound. Humans think in abstract terms, frequently using their minds to transport themselves to thoughts which are out of their physical reach. So, religious thinking is a basic human characteristic—being a direct part of our deep-thinking abilities.

Throughout the pages of this book, you will find religion has played an instrumental part in the development of human societies. In fact, my book takes this claim even further—declaring it is impossible for humanity to survive without religion.

As you read further, I am confident you will agree. The development and practice of spirituality throughout human history granted people an otherworldly inspiration to accomplish community goals, in addition to uniting people.

Throughout this book I will provide scenarios where you can see yourself through the lens of the ancient world—allowing you to grasp, perhaps for the first time, the incredible purpose of religious belief. So, as you continue reading, be prepared to gain understanding. Your worldview will be transformed.

So, how does *atheism* fit in with this?

In the atheist system, there are many in the 21ˢᵗ Century who deny God's existence. Some go much further—even deriding *all* forms of religions as mere fantasy.

However, once I show you the unreliability of atheism, your mind will be fully open to consider my later points. . . .

<u>Atheism Must Acknowledge the Supernatural</u>

Although atheism denies the supernatural—saying reality consists only of physical things—in its acknowledgement it indirectly acknowledges the presence of supernatural things.

French philosopher, Rene Descartes, once said, *"Cognito ergo sum"*—which means, *"I think, therefore I am."*

Now, an atheist may begin from a similar position as Descartes—saying he only knows his own thoughts. But this is a faulty position.

A *physical* brain can produce only *physical* things. Therefore, a physical brain could not determine ultimate truth, logic or reality beyond itself, because truth and logic are not physical things. In other words, we cannot measure "truth" or "logic." They are not chemical reactions in the brain. Nor are they something which can be weighed.

Therefore, even in an atheist's acknowledgement of himself in stating, "*I think therefore I am,*" he is demonstrating he is a physical being operating in a reality which is somehow supernaturally governed—beyond physical matter.

Consciousness is supernatural because it requires comparison. By a person acknowledging his own existence, he is evaluating the world around him—inferring he "exists in a conscious state" while other inanimate physical things do not. Frankly, this type of comparison is not the result of merely physical chemical reactions in the brain.

A brain produces only physical chemical reactions. But those physical chemical reactions are "sure" of nothing beyond the chemical reactions themselves. So, if a person acknowledges only physical matter, there exists no ability for the physical world to assess itself. Therefore, consciousness itself is supernatural.

Now, the common position of atheism is that "*consciousness is an emergent property of matter.*" In other words, this means that physical chemicals somehow develop the ability to think once enough of them gather together.

But in putting forth the idea that matter can *will* itself into consciousness, atheism reveals how it must rely upon concepts of things in reality which supersede physical matter—and are therefore "supernatural," while simultaneously working so diligently to deny the supernatural.

Do you see the conflict?

Atheism denies the supernatural, yet it relies upon supernatural things, such as consciousness, truth and logic. So, in a most bizarre fashion, when the atheist uses "logic" in the development of his thoughts against the supernatural, he must rely on the supernatural—because "logic" is something which exists independent of physical reality, being impossible to weigh or measure.

And, in this love-hate relationship, as atheism uses the supernaturalism it despises in the very arguments for their worldview, atheism manifests in its true form . . .

Insanity.

One cannot rightly declare physical matter is all that exists, while simultaneously using "truth," "logic," and "consciousness."

Atheism has No Basis for Truth or Logic

Moreover, if atheism denies the supernatural, it has no means to determine truth. Because, if the extent of my brain's operation is to merely produce chemical reactions, then any discussion would be nonsense.

Atheism provides no basis for truth or logic. Without these supernatural things, one is left to only view the physical chemical reactions of the brain. And this leads to absurdity. No matter how compelling, all "thoughts" would be mere physical chemical reactions—being impossible to compare to an external, supernatural standard such as "truth."

I'll state this another way . . .

If someone were to say something to you, you could measure what he said based on "truth" and "logic"—determining whether his statement matched your own observations of reality.

But, if one acknowledges *only physical matter*, there exists no reference point to assess a brain's thoughts. Therefore, an atheist's best thought is nothing more than a mere chemical reaction. So, in order for the atheist worldview to work properly, supernatural things like "truth" and "logic" must be smuggled in, while the atheist simultaneously denies the existence of anything beyond physical matter.

So, how does this apply to this book?

Well, when understanding the absurdity of atheism, and the fact that it has never worked long-term, it angers me to see atheism attempting to dissuade people from religion—which can explain "truth" and "logic," and has been used for countless generations to successfully organize human societies.

Moreover, it is most cruel for atheism to attempt to dissuade humans from religious belief, when religion has always been the primary means of humanity's survival. It would be akin to someone convincing a farmer to burn all his fields before he harvests his crops—dooming him to face winter ignorantly unprepared.

Thus, atheism is wooing humanity to destroy religion—in effect leaving us unprepared, with no time-tested method of overcoming tragedy. Surely, difficult times always visit human societies. And without religion, humans possess no time-tested methods of dealing with those tragedies. In this, atheism is a most fell venture, leading humans to forsake religion—the one thing which enabled their ancestors to survive.

Of course, however, humans in the 21st Century will have a difficult time understanding this. Perhaps it will be impossible for readers to understand. After all, if one has never experienced true, unrelenting, inescapable tragedy and suffering—like that experienced commonly in the ancient world—they are most ignorant.

So, if you approach this book in 21st Century ignorance, simply begin by acknowledging your ignorance as I have done. It is okay to admit your lack of understanding. And, once you acknowledge your lack of understanding, you can truly learn. Your mind can be filled with new thoughts and your worldview can be opened beyond your own perspective.

The problem, however, occurs when one is unwilling to acknowledge their ignorance as I have done. Therefore, I implore you as a fellow traveler. Set aside your pride and be willing to view your ancestors as they truly existed. Then you can begin to see clearly through all the falsehoods peddled by atheism in your generation.

Religion Actually Helps People Survive

If one is familiar with suffering, he can see within religion—no matter which one—the value in giving people hope and the ability to endure. When pressed, people either survive, or they do not. Of course, there is a time to discuss and contrast differences between various religions, but I will not be comparing religions in this book. My goal is to simply coach you from ignorance, making it clear that spirituality in general is preferable to atheism.

At the least we can be certain religion has been effectively used by our ancestors to survive incredible tragedy. Whereas, atheism is a fly-by-night charlatan, peddling his snake oil to ignorant buyers; religion sells time-tested practices used by our very ancestors. So, although the world has many charlatans of many types—some of which wrongly peddle in the name of religion—at least in the case of religion it actually has worked for people in the past.

In other words, let's say you are sick and in need of a cure. And, in this scenario you don't know any better—so you have two possible options. You can either try the same medicine which has been used to cure your parents, grandparents and great-grandparents. Or you can use a different medicine offered to you by a man who just arrived in your town.

Surely, your best option, by far, would be to use the same medicine which cured all your ancestors.

It is obvious. Indeed, you are genetically similar to your relatives, so whatever worked well for them has a high chance of helping you as well.

This is why doctors ask patients about their family history of illnesses. Therefore, the lives of our ancestors bear incredible relevance to each of us. We would be most wise to consider how they lived their lives—using their stories to offer insight on our own lives.

So, in the example of the two medicines above, both medicines could be called "snake oil." But, you are always better off going with the snake oil which has actually helped your ancestors rather than using a different "snake oil."

Now, you might not understand "how" the medicine cured your ancestors. But, that isn't the point. Your best bet would be to use the medicine which has helped your ancestors survive, because, in doing so, you will likewise have the best chance for survival.

And, by extension, this applies to religious belief. When we look back at human history, we see our ancestors were religious. So, it makes sense for us to accept the same medicine which helped them survive. It would not be prudent to forsake a medicine which has been proven effective by previous generations in your family. Likewise, you should carefully consider their beliefs and allow them to inform your own worldview.

No matter the condition of our relationships with our families, we can be certain we carry within ourselves part of all of them. Maybe we carry the "best" of our family, or the "worst," but nevertheless our past bears relevance on our lives.

So, perhaps a good place to start would be to consider the most honorable family members you have and the beliefs which have guided their good behavior. Although we all have family members who have done wrong, doubtlessly we all have someone who we could uphold as an example of right behavior. And, if for whatever reason you do not, religion offers you a different pathway: Through religion you can be adopted into a new brotherhood—where you can have spiritual brothers and sisters. Simply follow in the footsteps of a good man who has lived before you. And, in doing so, you can benefit from the faith of previous generations.

Therefore, we are all a product of the good which can be accomplished through religion—because through it our ancestors found the pathway to survival. And, apart from our religious ancestors, we obviously would not be here. Religion is indeed an inseparable part of us as humans. Religion is in our blood.

As it was for countless generations before us, religion is still the pathway to survival. At all costs we must never dissuade people from survival. I'll explain this another way . . .

Atheism's attempt to pull people from religion is akin to dissuading a man from taking extra supplies and fuel for a long journey in the wintery cold. To dissuade a man to leave behind his fuel can, when you know he will need it to survive, is a terrible cruelty. And, this is exactly what atheism does to the ignorant.

As a wayward siren, atheism beckons atop the rocks for humans to drift from the routes of their ancestors. And, as atheism draws the ignorant ever nearer, they are at once pulled by the currents into the inescapable tossing of the waves—intent on shipwrecking them on the jagged teeth under the waters.

So, what should you do?

Consider this . . . you are human.

Then, once you are convinced of your humanity, determine how your ancestors survived. In doing so, you will be brought to the stunning reality: Your ancestors built their lives upon religious beliefs.

As you read, think of your objections to religion, then set them aside as you ponder on each chapter of this book. Of course, you may know people who are religious with whom you do not agree. Or you may have misunderstandings about a particular religion. Here I am not addressing people who offer lip-service to religion but secretly live against the faith they profess. I am appealing to those who are otherwise in danger of shipwreck in the midst of the ever darkening, pestilent 21st Century sea. I am appealing to you—because you *can* be saved. It might be too late for others, but it is not too late for you. I want you to regain hope—to learn to see beyond the physical prison of this fallen world. So, in all cases, approach what I say with level-headed openness, and you will see humanity with clarity. Break free of the false perceptions of the physical world and learn to walk by faith, my friend.

Religion has served as the pathway used by all our ancestors. When beckoned by sirens in their lifetimes, religion helped them stay true—intent on moving forward on those ancient routes traced under the stars by their ancestors.

Here is my hope for you: Don't be beckoned toward the sirens atop the rocks. Although you hear their songs, do not allow those melodies to take your heart captive. Likewise, do not follow others who are guided from true paths by siren songs. They will lead you on paths which are not good—and their end is destruction.

Instead, consider the pathways which have helped your ancestors survive tragedy in their generations. This is how you can best prepare to face tragedy in your generation. Stay away from the currents which attempt to pull you for their own sake. Stay clear of the teeth moving to grind you from underneath the waters. Rather, set your sight on the stars—carefully staying on the course handed down to you from your fathers.

Don't forsake religion. It can help you survive. And in this way, you will accept your place among your devout ancestors. Atheism is an untested fad; but you have religion coursing within your lifeblood—being passed down from your innumerable ancestors.

I implore you, travel the sure path offered by religion. When tragedy strikes, religion will remain a true companion, granting you courage, strength and endurance in your time of need.

I will show you, my friend.

Throughout my book I will make it clear how religion preserved the lives of our ancestors—helping them to reach adulthood and have children of their own. The stories told in this book should be entertaining and heart-felt, mentally ushering you to the presence of those who lived before you. You will see the world through their eyes, and in this new vision you will see the incredible purpose of religion.

Section II

The Human Mind & Religion

2:
The Human Mind is a Supernatural Enhancement

Birds have wings. Wings allow birds to put space between themselves and the dangerous world beneath them. Thus, a bird is capable of separating himself from things on the ground by choosing to take flight.

Like birds, humans are also subject to dangers around them. Whereas other creatures have claws, sharp teeth and vicious capability; humans are remarkably tame in comparison. Humans are slow, fragile and incredibly weak when compared with animals.

So, how did ancient humans survive?

Buffers.

Think about it . . .
Just as birds use their wings to buffer themselves away from the dangerous world below them, humans use many methods to place buffers between themselves and the dangers of the world. Humans build houses to buffer themselves away from the dangers of the heat and cold. Humans use fire to process food—protecting their fragile systems from harmful bacteria.

Weapons are also used by humans as safety buffers. When a human is threatened, it is instinctive to reach for something which can be used as a weapon. In this case, a stick may provide the human with extra distance from a predator.

Get it?

Well, what happens when a human doesn't have a stick?

As we consider the answer to this question, we draw closer to understanding what it means to be human.
Sure, humans have nails, but we don't have claws.

We have teeth, but they are rather inferior when compared to the teeth of predators. Frankly there is nothing in the physical human form which would indicate why humans would survive—or did survive. In other words, in the midst of a physically violent world, the human creature is indeed "easy pickings" for animals— who are vastly stronger and much fiercer.

Even when we consider animals who are not predators—humans would be considered physically inferior.

For example, consider the skunk: A skunk might not be a vicious predator, but it has a major weapon at its disposal to dissuade would-be attackers. The spray of the skunk is a powerful deterrent—allowing the skunk to live a comfortable, meandering life, relatively unconcerned with other animals around him. So, the spray of the skunk is a tool he uses to survive. Apart from his spray, however, the skunk might be easy pickings for a predator. But, that one attribute dissuades all attackers from messing with him.

Similar to a skunk, a porcupine is also protected by an awkward physical enhancement. If threatened, the porcupine merely orients his behind toward an attacker— putting hundreds of dangerous quills between himself and a predator. A foolhardy predator may choose to continue his pursuit, however. But in doing so, the predator will become the author of his own pain—pushing himself into a most terrible situation. Thus, the quills of the porcupine are the physical enhancement which protects him from harm.

Animals can also use their size as a weapon. Think of a hippopotamus. Although it does not use claws, its incredible weight makes this behemoth a terrifyingly powerful creature. So, even in the hippo's case—where it might lack other physical enhancements or agility—the size of the hippo alone deters all would-be attackers from messing with him.

A giraffe, although appearing unprotected, is capable of strong kicks with its powerful legs. And, even more devastating, the giraffe's neck is capable of being swung like a mace—battering an attacker with an attack akin to hitting them with a tree.

Although mice may be small, their agility is an incredible enhancement—allowing them to elude predators. In this way, the mouse is similar to many other rodents. In addition to agility, the mouse also has a high reproductive rate—allowing mice who are caught to be rapidly replaced by the next generation.

Yes, no matter where we look, it appears animals all have their own schtick. Each animal has physical enhancements and abilities which enable them to survive in its environment.

But humans are different.

Sure, humans possess some *physical* enhancements, but usually they are far inferior to those of animals. Earlier we mentioned teeth and claws. Although human have them, they are a sorry version when compared to other animals such as wild cats and dogs. Humans have claws and teeth, but they are not capable of truly threatening anything or deterring a predator.

Yes, humans have muscles—but when compared to other animals, humans are very weak indeed. Perhaps "lethargic" would be a better descriptor. Think of the speed of a dog or cat when compared to a human. These animals can run circles around the average human.

And, if ever a human were to fight with an animal, the skin and bodies of humans are incredibly soft and tender. Whereas animals often have heavy fur or otherwise hardened skin which reduce the tearing of their flesh; humans do not.

Or consider "agility." Think of a human trying to catch a chicken in an open field. Frankly there is no way. And this simple test shows his agility is vastly inferior to most and nearly all other animals.

Now, how can we catch a chicken?

"Think about it."

To catch a chicken, a human needs to think ahead. He could corner it, then predict its next move. Or he could set a trap for it.

In this example we see the only real noteworthy characteristic of a human is his "mind." What the human cannot physically accomplish, his mind finds a way. And, this leads us to the conclusion . . .

The human mind is a *supernatural* enhancement.

In fact, the only way in which a tender, physically unimpressive creature like a human can survive is through something which is inherently non-physical.

The mind of the human allows him to break free of the physical world. Indeed, in the midst of a physical world, where the odds are stacked against his survival, the human mind is his only effective method.

For example, the human's lack of fur means he is susceptible to the cold of night and winter. So, he must visualize a solution to this threat. And, by thinking, the human arrives at the conclusion—building a house and using fire to heat it from within.

Humans also lack the hearty ability of digestion possessed by other animals. Whereas wild animals can eat rotting meat, humans cannot (or at least would be most unwise to attempt doing so). Moreover, humans have difficulty digesting certain foods. So, humans must "think" of solutions to these problems—especially during winter months when food is unavailable.

So, what were the solutions humans developed to address these problems?

Simple . . . humans "thought" of how to preserve food—through the use of salting, canning, smoking, refrigeration and so on. These methods allowed humans to stave off the development of harmful bacteria in addition to making it last longer.

Furthermore, humans "thought" of how to process food—removing husks and undigestible portions from plants. Then humans used fire and other methods to partially "digest" their food. Although a human has only one stomach, in essence he uses fire as his first stomach—rendering food into a more palatable form.

How else have humans learned to use their minds as weapons?

The examples are nearly endless. Arrows and firearms allow humans to keep their tender bodies further from animals who could harm them. Agriculture has allowed humans to stave off hunger in times of famine. And so on. Think of nearly every human advancement and within it you will see the "mind" played a key part.

All these examples point to a stunning reality . . . The most notable characteristic of the human is his "supernatural" mind. The mind of the human is capable of complex, abstract thinking. He can visualize how he will catch a chicken before he catches it. And in doing so, the human is thinking "supernaturally"—in a way which defies the normal means which governs the physical world. Frankly, there is nothing within the physical form of the human which indicates he, as a frail, lethargically slow creature, should be able to catch a chicken.

Yet, a human has caught a chicken.

Indeed, he has caught *many* chickens—as evidenced by the myriad chicken farms today.

So, one could easily conclude the most notable human characteristic is one which is strikingly non-physical—and hence seated firmly within the supernatural realm. Therefore, the thing which defines "human" is indeed supernatural by nature—allowing humans to visualize and shape the physical world with abstract thought.

Those who deny spirituality would be wise to consider this. Your ability to think abstractly is a "supernatural" ability—a testament of reality beyond the physical. Your mind allows you to supersede the vast physical enhancements of predators. Your mind allows you to find a way to supersede the natural world—and in that sense your mind is supernatural.

Indeed, there is much beyond our senses. Abstract patterns of human thought hint at the unperceived mystery which swirls around us. The unseen spiritual reality only emerges in brief glimpses on the physical dimensions of existence—much as a tesseract shifts and moves in different dimensions. Our abstract minds can give us glimpses beyond the limits of the physical veil around us—allowing us to see beyond the merely physical.

The human mind hints at the true spiritual nature of humans. The human mind merges the physical with the spiritual—consisting of a physical brain, yet capable of existing and speaking beyond it.

What is the proof that the human mind is more than just the brain?

In the physical world, humans can record their thoughts on paper—inscribing them in forms so they can be understood for countless generations. And, in writing, perhaps we see the most prominent example of human spirituality. Human thought exists in written language—independent of the human brains which once were used to write the words. Thus, the human mind is capable of bypassing restrictions of the brain itself. Millenia after the writer's physical brain is consumed with the long decay of the grave, his mind continues to speak clearly through his words penned on paper.

Therefore, when you are told by atheism that only physical things exist, you must laugh—most heartily.

In all cases, the human mind absolutely defies the physical world, abstractly solving problems as it routinely interacts with concepts far beyond the veil of the merely physical. Humans are supernatural beings—who only for biological necessity momentarily bear physical form.

And, even after humans set aside their physical form, they continue to speak through written word.

The continued survival of physically weak humans among a vastly stronger animal kingdom is a testament to the supernatural foundation of humanity. Apart from the human's supernatural capabilities, the human would be easy pickings for predators. Therefore, the only way in which humans have survived is through their supernatural capabilities.

And, the more abstract and supernatural the individual human, the more likely he would be to survive—developing solutions to problems which swallowed up the merely-physical-thinking men within his generation. In other words, religion further enhanced human creativity and imagination—spurring individuals to always see beyond the merely physical. So, throughout the countless generations of humanity, those humans who were the most religious were the ones with the highest chances for survival. But those who denied the supernatural became mentally handcuffed to the physical circumstances around them.

This is why all ancient human societies were religious. The more outlandishly creative and imaginative the human, the more likely he would be to develop solutions to problems.

Today, don't fall into the trap of thinking everything *physical*. There is much which occurs beyond our notice. In the physical world we lack understanding. How much more then do we lack in our understanding of what lies beyond the physical veils of our existence?

3:

Dreams & REM Sleep: The Fount of Supernatural Belief

It is clear humans think supernaturally. Humans are ever inclined to imagine and ponder things which are beyond their physical sight.

Of course, from my belief in the Bible, I am tempted to assert my own belief here—specifically that humans think supernaturally due to Adam and Eve's direct interaction with God.

I believe this to be so.

And, since God directly interacted with Adam and Eve, there is a desire buried deep within each of our psyches to have a similar connection with God. Thus, from a Bible perspective it is easy to account for the supernatural inclination of humanity.

Indeed, we are each "wired" to interact with God—so we all inherently desire supernatural things on some deep level. It is like each of us has a spiritual cord which desires to be plugged in. But, when we cannot find God, we nevertheless desire to be plugged into something (or anything) spiritual.

However, I will not discuss my Bible perspective further. Rather, I want to present this topic from a neutral perspective which can be generally accepted by *all* readers.

So, if one does not accept the Bible, how can the widespread supernatural beliefs of humanity be explained?

In other words, if humans are merely physical creatures, like other animals (as atheism supposes), then what would cause humans to imagine something apart from the physical world?

Why would humans begin to think of the afterlife, bury their deceased or practice religion in any form—if indeed humans are merely animals as atheism posits?

These are intriguing questions, compelling us to consider the very fount of supernatural human inclination.

So, why were ancient people so inclined toward religious, supernatural thinking?

Answer . . .
Dreams and REM sleep.

Let me explain . . .
As physical creatures, humans are immersed within a physical world. The world around us can be seen, heard, felt, smelled and touched. Thus, within a human's physical experiences he may develop the perception that there is no reason for him to think of anything "supernatural"—that is existing beyond the "natural."

However, dreams are the human's portal out of purely physical thought. Dreams are incredibly significant. They are the visions which wholly capture our minds during sleep. And, these dream visions are incredibly significant when we consider we spend one-third of all our time sleeping.

Therefore, dreaming must be upheld as perhaps the most significant aspect of our psyches. Or, I could go further in saying "dreaming is the primary physical function through which humans structure their entire worldview." The form of humanity, as it currently exists, has been impacted most by the function of dreaming.

Do you believe me?

I will show you . . .

Memories as Sense Snapshots

During our waking hours, the human brain stores snapshots of our senses at certain times throughout each day. Those snapshots become memories. Our memories are simply recordings of what we saw, heard, felt, tasted and smelled during a moment.

When we "remember" a past event, we are really just cycling through the sense data which was stored in that moment. In other words, a smell can remind us of a particular place because within that memory snapshot that particular smell is stored in association with what we also saw and heard at that moment.

For example, the smell of popcorn may remind me of a carnival. Upon smelling popcorn my mind makes it possible for me to "see" and "hear" the carnival because those senses are stored in association with the smell of popcorn.

Make sense?

This is a simple concept. Our minds do not store memories chronologically, but as sense snapshots. The only way we get chronology is when we consciously try to piece together the time-order of events. But frankly our memories are not chronological.

<u>Survival—The Purpose of Dreaming</u>

As a physical creature, your brain is most concerned with its *survival*. Remember this.

As creatures concerned with survival, humans *consciously* think in linear time. Each moment must be surpassed to get to the next.

But within the human *subconscious*—the realm from which dreams proceed—chronology and linear time are pointless. To our subconscious all that matters is we survived all past moments leading up to now. This is important to understand, and it bears relevance for our understanding of dreams . . .

As humans spend one-third of their time asleep, their subconscious minds constantly cycle through the "sense snapshots" they previously experienced. This results in a jumbling of different sense snapshots—which explains why our dreams are often a tangled mess of conflicting thoughts. This demonstrates our subconscious brains are not concerned with the chronological arrangement of memories. Rather, each memory exists as a sense snapshot.

So, our dreams would be best explained as a random, conscious viewing of loose photographs from our subconscious, rather than viewing photographs in an album. In their raw form, the photographs are not joined to one another. It takes effort for our brains to sort through them—and some of that sorting takes place when we are asleep.

Remember: The brain's chief concern is survival.

So, why do we dream?

Survival.

And why do many other physical creatures dream?

Also, survival.

I am sure we have all seen a sleeping dog who is "chasing rabbits"—as they hilariously snarl, snap and run while asleep.

Humans are very similar. While we sleep, our brains are *guessing*. Since our brains are concerned with survival, they realize sleep is a time where we are most vulnerable. As our bodies slow into their phases of rest, it is important our brains somehow keep us oriented to our "likely" physical surroundings.

How does the brain do this?

As we sleep our subconscious brains flip randomly through sense snapshots. By exposing us to a mix of random senses, our brains feed us a general *situational awareness*—which somewhat mirrors what *might* be happening around our bodies in the physical world.

Of course, our brains give priority to those sense snapshots which contain the greatest senses of arousal—because those are determined to be the highest survival priorities. This is why our dreams tend to stick on occurrences where we were frightened or joyful. Of course, our brains cycle through other sense snapshots which did not perk us up, but when they get to something significant our brains tend to stick on those thoughts in our dreams. This is all connected to survival.

Since my brain wants to survive, when it comes across a sense snapshot where a smell in one snapshot is similar to another sense snapshot where I was chased by a barking dog, then my brain will make me mindful of this in my dream. My subconscious brain simply examines the similarity in sense data, then leaves it to my consciousness to think chronologically to determine a cause and effect relationship.

For example, let's say one year ago I ate popcorn at the carnival. And shortly after I ate the popcorn I was chased by a dog—terrified I was going to be bitten.

Now, let's say before I went to bed today, I ate popcorn.

As I drift into sleep, my brain begins its examination of sense snapshots. As my brain examines the smell of popcorn, it may make the strong connection to the previous sense snapshot where I was chased by the dog.

Conscious & Subconscious Self

Because my brain is concerned with survival, it is in *its* best interest to warn me about that past experience. After all, if my body is killed, my "brain" knows it will also die. Therefore, my subconscious brain takes an active role in warning me about things which may have escaped the notice of my conscious mind. In other words, during dreams my brain is conducting a deep dive of previous sense snapshots to make sure something crucially important has not escaped my notice. Thus, dreaming is the means through which my brain brings forth sense snapshot data from my subconscious—parading various images before my consciousness.

If you are looking for an analogy, picture your "conscious" self as a king. Throughout the day, the king is involved with various tasks. But at the end of the day, the king takes his seat upon his throne, merely serving as a stationary host to those who arrive within his court. So, as the king sits upon his throne, many of the servants within his kingdom may arrive to entreat him on various matters—whether inquiring for justice, offering entertainment or arriving as couriers bearing messages from afar.

Dreaming is very similar—as one's *subconscious mind* moves in a parade to entreat the *conscious mind*. Just as the servants themselves do not make decisions requiring royal decree, so also the subconscious mind does not make effort to understand the "big picture" or figure out issues of chronology. Rather, the various subconscious messengers merely arrive—each with a different message. It is the left to the king to make decisions. Similarly, during dreams, the subconscious feeds a parade of sense snapshots to one's conscious mind—leaving the task of sorting to the consciousness.

Cool huh?

Now, back to the carnival, popcorn and dog scenario . . .

In this specific scenario, my subconscious needs to remind me that previously "*popcorn = dangerous dog.*" After all, my brain is not concerned with chronology. For all it knows, the previous dog could have been drawn in by the popcorn—because perhaps the dog wanted to eat the popcorn. But my subconscious mind does not dwell on such distinctions, and within the dream realm the only message is that "*popcorn = dog.*"

So, the alarming message in my dream could be a sharp feeling as if I am being chased. Thus, my subconscious is trying to use my dream to warn my consciousness. And, as the sense snapshot is ushered before my seat of consciousness, its message becomes clear . . .

"You ate popcorn, so watch out for the dog!"

As this dream moves before my conscious mind, and I awaken from the nightmare, I will gradually sink back into my physical surroundings. During the nightmare about the popcorn dog, I had a surge of adrenaline. I jolted aware, ready with the strength of Hercules to fight any beast near my dream-dazed body. But upon waking I find there is no popcorn beast nearby.

Then, my conscious mind is able to slowly dismiss the intense sensation of danger.

Last, I may even chuckle to myself—thinking about the absurdity of a popcorn beast, while also being mindful of my last experience after eating popcorn.

Why is this important?

Those who dream, survive.

Vivid dreams increase my chances for survival.
Survival is the goal. And my brain's ability to picture something not physically present gave me a surge of energy and jolted me awake. Of course, at this time there was no popcorn beast. But let's say there was one. . . .

If there were a "popcorn beast," this dream could have been a life-saver—prompting me to awaken before I could be attacked.

Let's imagine a different scenario . . .

Imagine an ancient man who likes to fish. One day after reeling in a wriggling fish, he was approached by a bear. Without warning, the bear charged him and the man narrowly escaped by quickly climbing out of the ravine.

Several weeks pass.

After a successful day fishing, the man gathered wood for a fire and ate some fish in his camp—setting aside the bones and fish guts a couple feet away.

Then, promptly after eating, the man drifted into a deep sleep next to the glowing embers of his campfire.

Sounds relaxing enough, right? . . . A full belly and a warm campfire.

But, is this man in danger?

Anyone who knows bears will tell you keeping fish guts in your camp has the potential to draw in a bear.

So, in this case, this ancient man's brain may use dreaming as a means to remind him about the very real danger associated with the fish guts near his sleeping body. Indeed, as the man's body lies motionless in a deep state of sleep, "dreaming" may be his last hope—his brain's last defense to ensure its survival through giving the man an intense reminder of his previous bear encounter.

In this case, the man's dream jolts him awake with a surge of adrenaline. He awakens with the sensation he is about to be chased by a bear. The man is sweating and breathing heavily—as if he were running in his dream.

In the brief seconds following his awakening, the man's mind reorients itself amid the cool evening air. His eyes vainly probe the deep darkness enveloping his camp. As his eyes pierce the darkness, the cool breeze upon his face and the shifting lights in the eerie blackness makes him feel incredibly small—and most vulnerable—within this void. All that remains of his campfire is now a faint glow at his feet.

Then the man "smells"—his nose detecting the slight odor of the fish guts a few feet beyond the fire.

In a stunning realization, the man suddenly remembers the previous fish and the bear chase. His conscious mind validates the danger connected to the fish guts. He springs up, removing the fish guts from his camp. He quickly returns to his campsite to tend his fire.

The spike in adrenaline brought on by the nightmare does not permit the man to drift back to sleep. So, he spends the remaining hours of the evening sitting quietly, yet fully aware, in front of his fire.

And, at the end, if the man has opportunity for full reflection, he will develop gratitude for his dream. In fact, his dream saved his life—awakening him mere minutes before the arrival of a bear lingering around his camp.

<u>Dreamers Survive; Non-Dreamers Perish</u>
Thus, we see the true purpose of dreams. Dreams allow our subconscious to grant profound situational awareness to our consciousness while our bodies are paralyzed in stages of deep sleep.

And, in turn, those ancient humans with the *most* vivid dreams would have been *most* prepared for the predators which lingered around their camps.

But those ancient humans who did not have vivid dreams were most susceptible to predator attacks. Therefore, one's ability to imagine—to think supernaturally in dreams—was a novel enhancement which increased one's odds of survival in an inherently dangerous world.

Did I make you a believer?

Do you see the importance of dreaming as the brain's measure to help a person survive?

In this way there is a direct cause-effect relationship between one's ability to imagine and his survival. The ancient person who can imagine a bear will always be mindful of bears. Whereas the ancient person who only thinks in terms of what is physically present may actually one day be killed by a bear.

Multiply this effect by hundreds of human generations and we quickly realize why all humans dream. Only the dreamers survived! And, since dreamers were the ones who survived, they had children of their own—who with each successive generation became much more likely of being vivid dreamers.

In ancient human history, there were indeed countless humans who didn't have such vivid dreams. And in the night those people were picked off by bears, leopards, lions or other predators who came upon them unaware. But the person who vividly dreamed developed a deep-seated wariness of all potential dangers. For that reason, humans who imagine things lurking just out of sight in the shadows are selected for survival.

Neat, huh?

Keep multiplying this effect over many years. Eventually we see the population of people with vivid dreams growing, while the number of people without such imaginations succumbing to beasts in the shadows. After all, to survive predators in the darkness, you must develop the ability to "see" them—even when your eyes cannot physically see them. Thus, within the dream realm, the human mind practices the most useful skill of imagination.

So, are thoughts of the supernatural really that fanciful?

Not at all. In fact, dreams are incredibly useful—and even vital for survival. Indeed, one's odds of survival are much better if they trust in their own dreams rather than the advice offered by atheism.

Spirituality and taking heed to dreams—however bizarre—can actually save one's life, just as dreams have saved countless humans before us. Remember, your subconscious brain wants you to survive. But atheism is altogether unconcerned with your survival.

So, no matter how absurd or imaginative, your dreams are your brain's best effort at ensuring its own survival. Therefore, you should take heed to your dreams—especially in situations which may be dangerous. Indeed, it is no wonder why ancient humans often associated dreams with the spiritual realm—for within these nighttime visions God could warn people of dangers beyond their physical perception.

<u>Weird Things in Dreams</u>
Within our minds, dreams are *real*.
Let's return to my scenario of the popcorn dog. . .

.

In my dream, I may have the sense I am being chased—as a result of the physical experience of getting chased by the dog long ago.

However, because my brain only remembers "sense snapshots," it truly is irrelevant what the imagined creature looks like within my dream. In fact, my brain may morph the physical dog into something completely different altogether. And, after all, this is what we would expect.

Why?

When I was chased by the dog after the carnival, what did my *physical senses* actually record? . . .
Only the following:
The *sound* of barking.
The *feel* of my bicycle beneath me.
The *smell* of popcorn.
The *feeling* of the Sun's heat on my back.
The *vision* of the road under my bicycle.
Feeling my heavy breaths and racing heartbeat.

So, considering the above, note I was not *staring* at the physical features of the dog. Rather, I was racing to get *away* from the dog. Therefore, within my "sense snapshot" memory of that event it makes sense the appearance of the creature chasing me may be warped. After all, within my brain's snapshot of that experience the exact physical appearance of the creature chasing me was irrelevant. My eyes only "recorded" sight of the road under my bicycle because I was not staring at the dog. Therefore, my nightmare connected to this event may in fact not at all represent the form of the beast who was chasing me because that data was not "recorded" in my sense snapshot.

Make sense?

Let's extent this principle further . . .

One-third of our lives are spent asleep. Generally, this means one-third of all our brain's thoughts will not directly correspond to the normal rules of the physical world.

I'll say it again . . . One-third of all your thoughts do not conform to physical laws.

So, it is no wonder why humans are so inclined to be religious. At our core, as creatures who dream and remember dreams, humans straddle the line separating the physical and spiritual world. And, just as physical world events influence dreams, it is logical for humans to infer that spiritual events in dreams also influence physical world events.

Simple.

Furthermore, when considering the development of supernatural thinking, it makes sense for humans to imagine creatures which vary in appearance from what we experience in the physical world.

In fact, my dream may manifest the barking creature as a dark cloud—perhaps conflating my *sight* of the blurring gray asphalt under my racing bicycle with the *sound* of the dog. So, whereas physical "dark clouds" do not chase us in our normal experiences; they certainly can chase us in our dreams! Thus, dreams become the fount of all supernatural thinking.

Thus, in the dream realm "sense snapshots" can be warped or combined with one another. Remember: Our brains' goal is to help us survive—staying in tune with potential risks which may exist just outside our immobilized, sleeping bodies. Our brains are not concerned with accurately representing the physical world because the rules of physics are irrelevant to the interplay between our subconscious and conscious.

Instead, our subconscious brains only give us what they determine to be a somewhat relevant mixture of different sense snapshots—providing us with a "mix tape" of things which happened somewhat recently or have especially strong feelings of arousal attached to them. By doing so, our brains keep us in a constant state of general situational awareness while our bodies are in deep stages of sleep.

Moreover, since the goal in dreaming is for our subconscious to elicit an emotional response within our consciousness, the images of dreams are much more effective if they are warped. Truly, your subconscious wants to give you warped images.

Indeed, a dark cloud has much more potential to create fear than a barking dog. Whereas a "point of reference" exists for a barking dog; no "point of reference" exists for a demonic dark cloud which chases people. In other words, we have all seen friendly dogs who bark—so a barking dog in a dream really is not that intimidating. After all, the dog could be barking as it is playing joyfully with another dog—and in that case there would be nothing to fear.

But, on the other hand, a demonic dark cloud which chases people is indeed fearful. No point of reference exists in the physical world for such a "creature" because no one has ever seen one. So, it is much more likely to cause fear within one's consciousness as the mind attempts to grapple with the bizarre vision being presented within the nightmare.

And, in this reality, one can clearly see the more bizarre and otherworldly the dream, the better the intended effect of evoking a strong emotional response in the consciousness of the dreamer. This is why ancient societies were all religious: Vivid dreamers dream vividly and those vivid dreams help them survive.

And the more vivid one's dream, the more it would stick with them upon awakening. So, it makes sense that religious meaning would be attached to such vivid dreams—which in turn encouraged more people in society to likewise share their vivid dreams. Over time, religions gained momentum as they provided a generationally-stacking contribution to societal survival:

Dreams increased individual survival and religions made people increasingly value their dreams.

Cool huh?

Body Paralysis During Sleep
Did you know your body actually experiences *paralysis* in REM sleep?

When your body moves into the deeper stages of sleep, your arms and legs are immobilized. In essence, your body shuts down many of its conscious connections. So, during these deep stages of sleep we are most vulnerable.

Interestingly, REM sleep is a stage of sleep where body paralysis is often accompanied with very vivid, emotional dreams.

Have you ever awakened suddenly, feeling like you want to laugh, cry, run, fight or do some other exciting activity?

Most likely this was a result of you awakening from REM sleep.

So, why would the human body give us such deeply emotional dreams while we are in a stage of body paralysis?

The answer is simple . . . Survival.

In the case of the ancient world, humans needed a dramatic startle reaction to accompany untimely awakenings. The flood of emotions experienced at these times would give humans the ability to instantly fight or flee from a predator. The vivid images associated with dreams in this stage give the conscious mind a stunning ability to instantly transition from body paralysis in a deep stage of sleep to fighting in the next moment.

In this way, the supernatural visions of the dream world—whether of dark clouds or whatever—actually saved the lives of many ancient humans.

But what became of ancient humans without this strong ability to dream and imagine?

Perhaps their dreams during these deep stages of sleep were less powerful. Over time, ancient humans who awakened from sleep paralysis with grogginess would have been the ones eaten by the predators. However, those humans with the ability to see the "dark clouds" of the dream world chasing them more readily would have always maintained a higher wariness and readiness to confront a physical predator whenever one emerged.

Therefore, within the context of dreaming, supernatural thinking is most useful.

And, the ability to form supernatural thoughts in the dream realm directly translated to a higher likelihood of survival in the case of physical dangers emerging during these times. There is a direct cause-effect relationship: The ability to imagine supernatural things in the ancient world yielded a higher likelihood of survival.

Over the course of hundreds of generations, humans with the most vivid imaginative abilities were the most likely to survive childhood, adolescence and to have children of their own.

<u>Dreams and Religion</u>

So, why were all ancient human societies religious?

Of course, if a dream allowed you to awaken at a critical moment, as a predator closed in upon your body, you would surely ascribe supernatural meaning to that dream—saying God or other supernatural beings warned you of danger, and delivered you. And, in those cases you might be correct.

When considering the deep emotional states associated with vivid dreams, it makes sense humans would ascribe religious meaning to such dreams—especially if a dream seemed to predict a certain event, or was perceived to have prevented tragedy.

Imagination was founded within dreams and further promoted by religion—thus becoming the most decisive survival trait of ancient humans. It gave them a general wariness and situational awareness which increased their likelihood of survival in cases of actual danger.

In the ancient world, a person who lacked imagination would be a sitting duck for any physical misfortune which could happen upon them as they were in the midst of sleep paralysis.

Therefore . . .
Vivid, supernatural dreams = survival.

Furthermore, religions make much of dreams—often ascribing divine purpose to dreams and visions. And, in this way, religion reinforced the importance of dreams—encouraging people to dream more, have visions, and to heed them with diligence. Therefore, the *most religious* people—who ascribed the most importance to dreams—were the most likely to survive, constantly being refined by their subconscious mind, carefully considering past events from different angles and seeking to reconcile their past experiences with one another.

Frankly, those who were less inclined to dream, or who did not uphold their dreams in a similar sense of religious reverence were much more likely to perish.

So, if you have vivid dreams, be encouraged! This is a testament of your ancestors' survival. You come from a long line of people who dreamed vividly—and were at many times saved from danger through their dreams. So, when atheism beckons you to abandon supernatural thinking, dwell on the importance of dreaming and your connection to the supernatural. Your spiritual imagination and ability to think supernaturally is a gift which should be embraced. And, in turn, your ability to dream can likewise preserve your own life in the way it preserved the lives of your ancestors.

In conclusion . . .

Vivid dreamers were more likely to survive.
Vivid dreams were ascribed religious meaning.
Religion fully embraces and encourages dreams.
Religion is better than atheism.

In the above pattern, we see religion works with dreams successfully. Dreams help people survive. Then religion upholds those dreams and encourages people to dream more. In turn this further increases the odds of survival for religious dreamers. And, over time, this is why the populations of religious humans continued to increase within human settlements—as religious humans dreamed and encouraged other religious humans to dream. Thus, the religion itself accelerates survival among adherents through their mutual encouragement of one another. This is a beautiful system which should be embraced as it promotes the well-being of individuals in communities.

But atheism beckons individuals to forsake the successful dream-based methods of their ancestors. Atheism encourages people to depart from spirituality—which has used dreams to save countless people throughout history. Atheism is a dull reliance upon only the physical; while dreams are limitless—capable of ushering us into the eternity of imagination.

Atheism is a boring declaration of physical borders—saying one can go no further than the physical.

But religion offers an unlimited transcendence of the physical—encouraging humans to move beyond through spirituality.

So, which one can take a person further?

Clearly, religion bears hope and promise; whereas atheism is an absolute dead-end—a stunning denial of the supernatural principles at work within humans as evidenced by the power of dreams.

Therefore, religion is better than atheism.

4:
Remembering Dreams

One-third of our lives are spent asleep. Generally, this means one-third of all our brain's thoughts will not directly correspond to the normal rules of the physical world.

I'll say it again . . . One-third of all your thoughts do not conform to physical laws. So, it is no wonder why humans are so inclined to be religious. At our core, as creatures who dream and remember dreams, humans straddle the line separating the physical and spiritual world. And, just as physical world events influence dreams, it is logical for humans to infer that spiritual events in dreams also influence physical world events.

Simple.

Humans dream and remember their dreams. Whereas other creatures dream; humans dwell on dreams. When we awaken, we can remember our dreams—and they continue to impact us throughout each day.

Not so with animals.

Now, you might have viewed your dog before chasing a rabbit in his dream, but when your dog awakens, he no longer pursues the rabbit. The dream leaves him as soon as he awakens.

However, humans remember their dreams—and these physically non-existent realities continue to mold and shape events far after they were retrieved by the subconscious mind during sleep. It is common for humans to have dreams which are so intense that the emotional arousal from the dream sticks with the individual throughout the entire day. Some human dreams are indeed so vivid and profound that they serve to inspire lifelong change.

Have you had such a dream?

It is likely you have.

Have you ever dreamt something so vivid that the emotion aroused by the dream stuck with you for hours?

It is likely you have.

This ability of humans to "remember dreams" makes them distinct from animals. And within this unique human characteristic is found the spiritual inclination of humanity.

To extend this thought further, the human life is in fact a "physically enhanced dream." Think about it. . . .

We spend more time within our own minds than we do outside of them.

We think in pictures.

Throughout each day our minds constantly play through coming events.

And, in these ways, humans spend much more time in a dream-like state than they do as a physical creature within physical reality.

So, humans are indeed vastly more spiritual than they are physical. Although we have physical bodies, the consciousness of humans finds its place interacting with abstract "non-physical" things which are not presented to any of their senses in that moment.

In other words, you can be standing in a grocery store line, but in your mind you are cooking. Or you can be sitting in church, but in your mind you are thinking about your garden. We should not lose sight of how profound this part of our nature is.

Dogs and other animals do not do such things. A dog who is in your backyard is "in your backyard." A dog who is eating, is immersed in the physical task of eating. However, humans do not totally exist within their physical circumstances. No matter where the physical body of a human may be found, his mind has the capability to be anywhere it desires.

Do you get it?

Another way of putting it . . .

A dog is concerned with his surroundings—being totally immersed in what his senses are experiencing in that moment. A dog does not think about what he will be doing in an hour, but humans do.

In fact, humans are consumed with such thoughts—which pull us to far-off places and events throughout each day even as our bodies are firmly tethered to the physical reality in which they exist.

But what is it that makes the human brain so different from the brains of animals?

The human mind is an eternal well-spring—capable of ever shifting and moving independent of the physical body which holds its brain. In this way humans are most notably different than animals. Humans exist and flourish within imagination.

And, when we consider the abstract mind of a human, perhaps the imagination is the most notable touch-point of the spiritual human nature. Our bottomless capacity of imagination beyond our physical circumstances is indeed an integral part of human nature.

Now this is not to say those humans with less imagination are "less human." Or, in the maximum application of this thought, that those who are incapacitated and thus lacking imagination are "non-human." Rather, the inherent "potential" of imagination is itself a part of human nature—even in cases it does not fully develop due to incapacitation.

Moreover, as I discuss in my other books, human nature itself exists independent of its physical body. Our imaginations prove we are not simply the product of our senses and physical bodies. A human routinely moves beyond and away from their body in thought. And, as I explain elsewhere, when the physical human body dies, it is this spiritual, imaginative part which is disembodied and resurrected by God. This is an interesting concept, so please excuse the red herring.

Back to the topic . . .

Humans remember their dreams. This simple characteristic is an important part of our nature. "Remembering our dreams" encourages us to continue "dreaming" throughout each day. This could easily account for the awakening of humanity—regardless of the worldview from which it is approached.

Think about it this way . . .

For a moment, let's assume humans were at some point in the past mere "physical" animals, lacking spiritual capability—like all other animals.

One morning, upon awakening from sleep, a certain human remembers his dream. In his dream he saw a giant mountain and he was running toward it. At the end of his dream he arrived at a spring of water near the base of the mountain. In his dream the man drank deeply from the refreshing mountain well. Then he awoke.

Let's imagine this is the first man who successfully "remembered a dream." And, upon awakening, he is shocked and amazed at the surge of emotions and the feelings within him as he slowly opens his eyes.

How do you think the man would interpret his experience?

Truly, the dream itself is supernatural. Although his brain was involved in the process, maintaining a dream upon awakening becomes supernaturally significant. The man's dream inspires him to see something which he cannot see with his physical eyes: the mountain and the spring. And although he may never find either the mountain nor the spring he can still just as truthfully taste the refreshing spring water within his mouth—refreshing him inwardly, deep down to the roots of his spirit.

Then, in a most profound fashion, the dream can become more "real" than the man's actual physical circumstances. This profound dream reality which he holds within his mind can be so inspiring it drives him to gather his belongings to trek out in search of the physical mountain which corresponds with the mountain of his dream.

> You must decide . . .
> Is such a powerful dream supernatural?
> Is it spiritual?
> Is it "real?"

The answer is subjective. In the determination of whether it is "real," it doesn't matter what skeptics think of the man's dream. They can naysay his dream as much as they desire, but if it is relevant and inspiring to the man then it is "real" to him. The man's dream—which inspires complete life change—is in fact more "real" than anything physical in his surroundings. The trees around the man may each bear physical form, but those things with physical form are not as capable of guiding him for his entire life. In other words, the mountain and the spring can become more "real" than anything which the man physically experiences.

Interesting, right?

So is the man's dream "real?"

Absolutely.

Is it relevant?

Yes.

Let's imagine this man lived in a desert region where water is scarce. Upon remembering his dream that morning, the man could interpret his dream as a vision granted by angels—guiding him to a better life.

As the man gathers his belongings and sets out in search of the mysterious physical mountain which matches his dream, he is compelled forward, being unshakable from his deep subjective reality. If he believes his actions are guided by a higher supernatural power, he will hold resolutely to the course ahead—no matter how difficult it becomes.

On the man's journey he may encounter many hardships which tempt him to abandon his mountain quest. But the man who "remembers his dream" anchors himself to an immovable vision of his future. The man who at first fixed his mind on the angels who granted the dream is also capable of imagining angels on his path who strengthen him along the way.

Thus, the man's dream grows more deeply relevant and powerful through his religious beliefs. Over time, as the man perseveres hardship, the dream becomes more "real" to him.

The man now becomes capable of feeling the angels' strength guiding him further in his journey. When he awakens each day, he does so with a renewed vigor—eagerly approaching each day with supernatural strength.

Now, at this point in the man's spiritual journey, he is growing ever stronger through hardship. His difficulties on the path compel him to move ever deeper within his faith—making the dream a part of his own fabric. He now sees himself as being guided by the angels—perhaps for a great purpose of discovery to be shared with others. And, with each step of his quest, the man's supernatural thinking makes him more resolute, courageous and powerful.

Have you ever wondered at the great accomplishments of ancient people?

A human who thinks himself a mere physical animal stops along the path when he encounters hardship. But a person who "remembers dreams"—thinking himself empowered by angels and guided to the accomplishment of a dream-declared task—becomes so inspired he would rather die than abandon his assigned course.

This is the power of religion.

Those who lack spiritual beliefs fall short of their goals. This explains why human history shows us no flourishing atheist cultures. However, those with the ability to fix their minds upon supernatural things gain the ability to press forward despite hardship. This explains why all ancient human societies who survived long-term were religious. A culture needs religion to survive hardships they encounter on the path to accomplishment.

Without religious beliefs stemming from remembered dreams, there is nothing to anchor humans in community when they encounter difficult times. Thus, all successful ancient societies were guided by those who were religiously guided by dreams. Those who "remember dreams" and assign them spiritual significance find the strength to endure difficult times. But "lack of religious belief" leads to "lack the resolve" when times are tough.

This is why all ancient human societies were religious. Only the most religious persevered. All successful human societies needed supernatural dreamers to guide their society. Today humanity still falls under the same principles which governed all societies in our ancient past. Human societies need religion.

History teaches us this most valuable lesson: Without religion, societies collapse. Period.

$\underline{5}$:
Sensory Deprivation

Suppose you find yourself in an empty room in an abandoned house. The windows and doors are shut—causing an eerie silence to settle around you.

Now imagine you were to remain in that room for several hours . . . maybe even overnight.

Even the most stout-hearted warrior may begin to feel spooked!

Why?

Our senses are wired to receive constant data from the area around us. Our minds receive a constant flow of data from our eyes and ears, in addition to what we feel, taste and smell. The brain arranges this data—providing us with a snapshot of where our body is currently located.

But, if our body is within a darkened, silent room, something happens . . .

Being deprived of the sense data to which it is accustomed, our brains *must* "guess" what is happening around our bodies.

Why?

The darkness and silence of the room may contain a predator—who is lurking, waiting to pounce on us at the opportune moment.

Those humans who were eaten by predators did not have further opportunity to produce offspring. Hence, we are all humans who come from those humans who *did* survive darkness—whether dark rooms, dark caves or dark forests.

We are the descendants of a long line of humans who *always* survived predator attacks.

Neat, right?

Therefore, we have inherited the same vigilance from the generations before us.

When our brains do not receive normal data from our eyes, our brains give us "guesses" at what "might be" lurking in the darkness. This is very similar to the dreams of REM sleep—in a way at least—in that the sleep paralysis of the body requires the subconscious brain to produce images (or dreams) to feed us with sensations to prepare us for the likely physical reality we may encounter if the delicate bubble of our sleep is shattered.

Likewise, in darkness our brains feed us with general anxiety designed to keep us on our toes in the case that a predator was to emerge from the murkiness which envelops our bodies.

So, why are *you* scared of the dark?

Because you are a descendant of those who survived darkness.

Your brain imagines creatures moving in the darkness to intentionally feed you anxiety. After all, those with the highest anxiety in the darkness will be most prepared to face any threat which emerges within it.

In darkness our brains can feed us the sensations of hearing voices or sounds—all for the purpose of increasing our chances for survival. Our skin may feel hypersensitive and the hair on our arms may stand—poised to detect the slightest shift of air around us, giving us increased time to slink away from a looming predator.

73

In other words, if one's brain is not receiving the sense data to which it is accustomed, it simply fills the gaps.

Thus, we see the blessed contribution which "superstitions" have granted to our survival. All ancient humans who survived were superstitious—being the most inclined to evade predators through hypersensitivity during times of vulnerability. And, superstitious people often take things even further—developing spiritual stories of supernatural beings to further inspire one another to remain safe amid danger.

In the ancient past, the sights and sounds borne from sensory deprivation in the darkness were interpreted as supernatural occurrences. And, as supernatural occurrences, it was common for people to develop superstitious tales about the darkness and the bizarre beasts which lurked within.

Yet, there were actual monsters who lurked in the shadows—large cats and wolves, but monsters nonetheless.

Each predator—whether physical or imagined—desired to consume ancient humans. So, in their superstitions ancient humans both protected themselves and adequately represented the sinister animations which ever sought to pounce from the shadows.

Sure, there might have never been "monsters" to be precise. But if the tales of monsters prevented the loss of life from predator attacks then all the tales accomplished their most useful purpose. Thus, it is better to have monster tales if the monster tales save the lives of your people.

After all, an ancient clan would suffer in many ways if its population experienced losses. Specifically, the loss of a young man would mean one's clan had less manpower to defend and provide for itself. And the loss of a young woman would mean one's clan would lack in its ability to produce more soldiers to defend the clan. So, the unnecessary loss of life was something to be avoided at all costs—because a small clan needed people so it could remain viable among other competing clans.

Get it?

Thus, in order for the members of the ancient clans to protect themselves they needed to protect one another. Remarkably, the best way to influence true, lasting behavior from which one will not dare stray is by teaching them a compelling superstitious tale. And if your "monster" is believable you can ensure the survival of your kin. But if your superstitious tale is unconvincing it will not produce fear—and eventually your clansmen may be picked off by monsters in the dark.

So, why were all ancient human societies religious?

Because the best monster stories were the ones which saved lives!

Those who lacked religion lacked imagination. As a result, the un-religious leaders created "dry," uninspiring tales which were ineffective at convincing clansmen to remain away from the dangers of darkness. And, over time, the numbers within non-religious clans dwindled as the populations of the most imaginative, interesting religious clans grew.

So, why should you be religious today?

Because it is interesting.
Because religion adds flavor to the dullness of the physical world.

Who wants to believe in only what they can see?

Yuck.

I want to use my mind to its fullest ability—and that involves the use of my dreams, imagination and spirituality. Anything less would rob me of my full measure of humanity.

Don't clip the wings of a bird.
Don't clip the mind of a human.

So, tell me your best monster tale!

I will not hinder your imagination.

And if your tale is most convincing it may persuade me to remain away from the darkness.

By telling a good tale within one's clan it minimized losses and injuries—thereby making the most imaginative and superstitious clans more viable among other clans. Eventually the clans with the best tales grew beyond the populations of those clans with the dry, unimaginative tales.

In other words, superstitious tales about monsters are vastly better at building societies than tales about merely physical things. This is why all ancient human societies were religious. Those who are superstitious tell the best tales. Those who are superstitious are much more adept at influencing behavior of citizens.

So, if ever you are planning to build a society, make it a religious one. Atheist societies do not endure long term.

<u>6</u>:
PTSD Dissociation

Of course, one may be tempted to think ancient religious leaders were swindlers—intentionally peddling untruths for personal gain, whether financial or social. However, let me dissuade you from this presumption by offering perspective on the ancient world . . .

In the ancient world, people encountered regular tragedy and trauma. The common trauma experienced was incredible—especially when viewed from a 21st Century perspective.

For example, siege warfare was one of the most common military strategies in the Ancient Near East. Essentially, an army would attack a city by surrounding it. In siege warfare the attacking army would stop supplies from entering. The attacking army would also prevent citizens from leaving.

Moreover, if a stream of water flowed into the city, the attacking army would attempt to block or divert the stream—even denying access to water. Then they would actually starve the people into submission.

In the Bible a detailed description of siege warfare is presented in the book of Lamentations—where it describes the horror of humans eating their children to stave off starvation.

Need another example of ancient world trauma?

Consider what life would be like in a world without police or emergency personnel at your immediate beckoning. The ancient world was remarkably brutal—where physical force was often the only law. Those with the strongest armies could do whatever they desired. And there was no one who could challenge the powerful.

Period.

When considering the above, it is disturbing to hear 21st Century humans who are critical of the patriarchal societies of the ancient world. Indeed, 21st Century criticisms serve only to reveal the critic understands nothing of the circumstances faced by our much stronger, ancient ancestors.

Let me pose this as a question . . .

Imagine you live in an ancient world where there are no police, what would you do for protection?

Think about it.

The more you think about it, the more you will begin to understand the Bible and other ancient books.

Living in a world without police would mean you would have to provide your own protection. Regardless of your moral objections, you would be *required* to fight for your family's protection.

Imagine you have a small farm. At any minute a raiding army of 100 men could descend on your family to rape and enslave your family, kill you, and take everything you owned—leaving only your burning hamlet in their wake.

Could you defend it on your own?

No.

So, what would you do?

You would obviously need to form an alliance with other farms.

But just having an alliance would not be sufficient to fight 100 raiders. Therefore, your alliance would need to form some sort of clan leadership to train your people to fight.

Now we are getting somewhere . . .

Keep thinking.

When facing the potential danger of 100 raiders, you would need men—not women—to all serve in your clan's army. (Frankly, women would be too valuable to lose—because each young woman could have many sons who in turn could further populate your army and working force.) And, to lead all those young men, you would also need a strong man—whom the other men intuitively fear and follow.

After all, physical combat is not for the faint hearted. You cannot simply "tell" a young man to fight for you. When the terror of combat seizes a person, everything within his brain tells him to flee. Courage is not a natural act—it is something which needs to be formed within young men by a strong leader.

So, if you have a large group of cowardly fighters there is no way they would be able to defend your village against raiders. An army of cowards is a vain hope. And when your family's survival depends on your army, you cannot leave anything up to chance.

Thus, the leader of the clan must be assertive and powerful—capable of inspiring those who follow him. After all, the only way to keep cowards on a battlefield is to train them to the point where their confidence overtakes their cowardice.

Remember this.

And the only way to dissuade men from fleeing battle is if they fear their clan leader more than their adversary.

Remember this as well. If you do, the Bible will begin to make sense to you.

Therefore, in the ancient world, patriarchal societies were the ones which survived. A clan needs a strong man in charge whom other men fear. He must punish the cowardly and train all the clansmen to be confident and effective in their fighting abilities. This means a successful ancient society will need young men to serve in the army and women to give birth to them.

Thus, a man is a most desired commodity—and each individual man puts your clan one step further from destruction. Each additional man within your clan means you have one more person to defend your village— therefore granting you an ever-thickening wall of protection against would-be attackers. After all, the alternative to this ancient patriarchy is your total annihilation—rape, pillage and burning.

Surely in the ancient world there were those who decried warfare and refused to fight. But what happened to those people? The answer is obvious: Clans which were led by strong men who led other strong men eventually destroyed those weaker communities.

Sad, but true.

Thus, as we examine the records of ancient history, we see that "natural selection" eventually weeded out all human societies which did not conform and find their place within this model.

Can you find perhaps a couple ancient societies which were different?

Sure, but it doesn't dismiss the fact:
Patriarchies = survival.

If you want to survive in the ancient world, put a strong man in charge who inspires fear and can effectively train young boys to be courageous, confident fighters.

If you *do not* want to survive in the ancient world—dooming your family to rape, pillage and burning—then stray from this patriarchal model.

When understanding the brutal dynamics facing competing clans, ancient morals come into focus. Anything which halted or slowed the production of men—who could serve as fighters and workers—was taboo. Therefore, in the most notable example, homosexuality became taboo in these cultures because homosexuality halted the sexual production of more fighters. And, whenever the production of new fighters was halted or slowed a clan began to grow increasingly more vulnerable to military threat from rival clans.

Like I said, reflect on the brutality of the ancient world and suddenly the morals developed in these societies make sense. Rules were not made to stifle free choice. Rather, rules were made to allow clans to survive amid an increasingly competitive world where rival clans ever sought expansion.

Simple.

Now that we discussed some of the terrible dynamics faced by ancient humans, we can re-address the original question posed at the beginning of this chapter:

Were ancient religious leaders mere swindlers— intentionally peddling untruths for personal gain?

Of course, there were certain situations where ancient religious leaders invented tales which they knew were not true.

This is obvious.

There are always people who make up falsehoods in an attempt to trick people. I will discuss this later in more detail.

However, I believe it much more likely that many supernatural beliefs were developed as a result of PTSD (also known as post-traumatic stress disorder). When ancient humans encountered trauma, their brains changed their perceptions in order to survive. This is a concept altogether foreign to people who are comfortable within the 21st Century—with the only exception being people who have encountered real personal tragedy, such as combat, brutality, violence, etc.

Please allow me to explain . . .

Imagine being stuck within a horrific place where you cannot escape. This was the exact situation faced by people within besieged cities (as we discussed earlier). They either died or somehow found a way to survive. Over the unrelenting weeks of trauma, eventually the person's mind shattered.

So, when people survived such situations, they did so through PTSD dissociation—where their mind developed the ability to "separate" their consciousness by depersonalization or derealization. In my book, Dear David: Learning to See God through PTSD, Anxiety and Depression, I explain this further. Although the person's body remained stuck within the situation, his mind "removes" him from it.

Thus, it could be simply stated, that religious belief is a vast enhancement to humanity. Those who developed the ability to perceive and believe in a reality beyond their horrific physical circumstances, survived. Yet, humans who could see only the physical world around them were lost to wither away within their own despair. Remarkably, a person with PTSD dissociation has the ability to be consciously transported to paradise—regardless where their body remains.

So, the ability to "see" supernatural creatures, like angels or whatever, is a part of this necessary survival enhancement for humans. Those who could supernaturally "see" beyond the horrors of the siege were capable of psychologically surviving it; whereas a person who senselessly objected to the supernatural would have despaired within it. And, once the "will to live" is gone within one's mind, his physical body soon thereafter follows its lead. But a person who readily accepted and believed in the supernatural maintained his "will to live."

It is interesting to think, but something as simple as a person "seeing" supernatural goblins around them helping them by bringing them invisible food, might have been the only thing which enabled a person to survive an extended siege.

Therefore, when we examine human history, we see humans were all religious.

Sure, there were some who, like atheists in the 21st Century, senselessly objected to all thoughts of the supernatural—refusing to even see the kind goblins who brought them invisible food. But those atheist-type people rarely survived. Over the course of hundreds of human generations, "natural selection" eventually dwindled the number of people who were genetically pre-disposed against supernatural thinking. This is exactly why religion is ubiquitously connected to all ancient human records. Without supernatural thinking (no matter how absurd), humans do not survive long-term.

In other words—no matter how laughable to consider—those people who imagined invisible helpful goblins were the ones who survived, but the people who could not or would not imagine such "ridiculous" things perished under waves of despair. And, in this way, a psychotic break within the minds of these survivors ended up being an absolutely critical benefit. Apart from the psychotic break achieved through dissociation an individual would be altogether abandoned to despair.

So, "losing one's mind" many times over resulted in "saving one's life."

It is a bizarre statement, but true—no matter how difficult it may be for readers to accept. The human mind is created to fold under certain pressure, re-shaping itself into a form which best fits its surroundings. Like an automobile transmission the human mind is capable of operating in different gears. PTSD dissociation is one of these common "gears."

What of those with absurd supernatural beliefs—like those who believed in goblins who brought them invisible food?

My conviction is the majority of ancient religious leaders were not swindlers. Rather, many ancient religious leaders had PTSD dissociation. They actually "saw" supernatural things, and their teachings simply relate what they experienced for themselves.

In other words, through dissociation, it is likely many religious leaders actually "saw" supernatural things. Then they re-told their experiences to others. Thus, many religions—no matter how outlandish—likely have roots in actual visions "seen" by religious leaders through dissociation or some type of trauma-induced psychological break.

Therefore . . .
Supernatural thinking = survival.

In the ancient world, those without "supernatural vision" were doomed to perish in tragedy—having no ability to effectively cope with their situations.

Supernatural thinking = will to live.

At times when our physical situations are dire, belief in the supernatural gives the person the ability to see beyond despair.

Supernatural thinking = inspiration.

So, what if a religious leader did not personally suffer tragedy?

When considering ancient religious leaders, perhaps their most notable shared quality was "discipline." Ancient religious leaders would fast—going without food for long periods of time. They often had the ability to reflect deeply in prayer or meditation. Many of them had wilderness experiences—where they persevered through a time of deep self-reflection preceding their teaching. And, ancient religious leaders directly confronted the physical world—challenging followers to see beyond their own physical circumstances.

In other words, whenever a religious leader lacked a personal suffering experience, he could intentionally afflict himself with suffering—disciplining his mind, perhaps even to the point of achieving a dissociation effect.

Think about it . . .

Ancient religious leaders often endured solo wilderness experiences—which would be akin to suffering a tragedy and learning to cope with it psychologically. They all fasted—which involved the denial of food, which was often a dynamic faced in ancient tragedies. And, the ancient religious leaders would often confront the materialism of the physical world.

Indeed, all these things serve as a profound blueprint for how humans can survive trauma. In the midst of an ancient world, it is no wonder why these people served as models to others. It is only through supernatural thinking one gained the ability to survive tragedy.

Ancient people, who understood this, would *practice ahead of time those disciplines of fasting, self-reflection and aversion to the comforts of the physical world.* Then, when the religious person was confronted with actual tragedy, they would have been prepared— perhaps already having achieved the requisite dissociation ability necessary for trauma-survival.

In other words, *religion was necessary in helping people to develop the mental ability to endure in the midst of trauma.* Similar to a vaccine, the practice of religion offered a time-tested mental immunity to the despair associated with ancient trauma.

This is why all ancient societies were religious.

My motivation in writing this book is to provide a mediation between ancient humans and 21st Century atheism—which tends to disparage and sneer at ancient humanity, deriding them as superstitious, "ignorant goat herders."

But I actually favor ancient humanity—far more in fact than 21st Century humans.

Why?

Ancient humans were survivors—being capable of using their imaginations to overcome absolute horrors. Moreover, I owe to them my gratitude and sincere reverence—because apart from their religious beliefs, humanity would not exist today.

In comparison, however, 21st Century people are dopamine-addicted, sloppy, undisciplined descendants of their much stronger, spiritual, physical-world denying, surviving ancient ancestors.

Somehow, the atheism which was "naturally selected" out of humanity in the ancient past has once again afflicted 21st Century humanity. The "comforts" of the 21st Century have once again beckoned forth atheism like a cursed Nephilim of the past.

Be warned . . .

In 21st Century humanity's quest to set aside the spiritual, they will create a future humanity incapable of survival.

Without religion, societies do not survive.

Even if, in your assessment, the religious people of the ancient past were "wrong," you nonetheless owe your life to them.

Even if you determine ancient religious zealots to be "insane" or "delusional," it was their supposed psychological insanity which purchased for humanity the generations which were born after them.

As a critical bane to 21st Century atheism, this fact must be brought to mind . . .

Religion was the way ancient humans survived.

7:
Despair
& The Will to Live

Very few of us have been trapped . . . truly trapped.

When stuck in an inescapable situation, the person is left with two options: (1) despair, or (2) find the "will to live."

In Viktor Frankl's book, Man's Search for Meaning, he notes the importance of a person's will to live. Once a person loses his determination to survive, he begins fading into an eventual physical death. However, if the person finds a way to re-conceptualize his physical reality, he can find the will to live.

Continuing my example from the previous chapter, I admit Viktor Frankl would not advocate for imagining invisible goblins who bring a starving person food. But I put forth the idea that it was such thoughts (no matter how absurd) which can be credited for ancient human survival. When pressed by unrelenting physical trauma, the humans who survived were the ones who were capable of imagining "supernatural" things. Thus, religious thinking allows a person to trade despair for hope—somehow "seeing" blessing in the midst of overwhelming suffering.

Do you understand?

If you do, this understanding of human trauma makes sense of ancient religions and even the most outlandish mythologies.

Whereas it is a trend amongst 21st Century critics to tear apart ancient religious beliefs; it was those "absurd" beliefs which enabled human survival. Of course, there were many ancient humans who were not inclined to imagine invisible goblins. But all such non-imaginary, physical-only thinkers were eventually lost to despair amid unrelenting ancient trauma.

This reality changes our understanding of ancient cultures. At first you may have been inclined to think "invisible goblins" ridiculous—but then again you are likely well-fed, living in safety and ease.

But if I were to remove your food and place you in a situation where you were brutally oppressed day after day, with no one to rescue you, then invisible creatures may indeed become your only hope.

As you sit in hunger and horror, eventually your mind is ushered to its breaking point—where you either (1) choose to fade in "despair" to exhaustion, or (2) find the "will to live" through a psychotic break or dissociation.

If it is the first, the pathway of despair ends only in decline and physical death.

But if it is the latter, your mind becomes capable of refreshing itself through its ability to imagine invisible creatures. Although the bars of your physical prison remain the same, your mind develops the ability to transform your perception within your physical cage. Your mind perceives the movement of the invisible creatures. Your mind focuses on each bite of the invisible food. You work to understand the goblins' language and behavior. Before you realize it, your mind shifts its focus out of its hunger—as you begin to imagine stories about the goblins.

As your subconscious begins placing these images within your consciousness, a beautiful process is taking place. Your subconscious is suppressing your feelings of despair by shifting your consciousness out of its physical circumstances. Your mind has shifted gears— transforming its perception of reality in order to allow you to survive the impossible. Therefore, psychological breaks and dissociation are in fact blessed survival capabilities. Of course, they are not compatible with 21st Century culture, but in an ancient world rife with inescapable trauma, those whose minds were equipped with multiple "gears" were the only ones who survived.

Do I have your attention?

Can you understand?

The whole point of religion is this . . .
To Survive Trauma.

Those who can "see" spiritual things are able to retreat from the trauma they are experiencing. This is a blessing indeed.

The ability to think supernaturally—to imagine— is the greatest enhancement of humanity.

Period.

Birds have wings. With their wings birds can move above the dangerous world below them. They make a buffer zone to separate themselves from predators on the ground. At any time they are threatened, birds can take flight—immediately separating themselves from the physical reality on the ground. Then, from its soaring heights, the bird chooses for itself when it will move into the physical world below it.

Pay attention to this.

Birds have wings. But humans have the inherent ability to transport themselves anywhere they desire, regardless of where their bodies may be stuck. The mind of the human is like the wings of a bird. Humans with the ability to "walk by faith, not by sight" can choose at will to soar above the physical world. Then, as the mind of the human soars, it chooses when it will move into and out of the physical world around its physical body.

This is exactly how a human's mind works. Although my body may remain stuck, my mind can soar out of its physical circumstances. This occurs as the subconscious mind toggles our consciousness.

Of course, to the person who has lived always in ease and comfort, this makes no sense. So, it is natural for a comfortable person to maintain a naturalistic worldview—where they uphold physical things as being the only things which exist.

However, I posit the true human condition is found within trauma. When a human is starving, broken and beyond hope in the physical world, then they can realize the full potential contained within them.

An atheist is like a flightless bird—with wings they "choose" to never use. After all, when life on the ground is comfortable, what purpose is there in flying? Thus, in the 21st Century, humans have indeed become disabled, wing-less birds—all content within ease and comfort, oblivious to the loss of their true spiritual form. Indeed, humans have been denied their spiritual nature for so long, they have altogether lost sight of the potential contained within their own minds.

Even the most spiritual humans fall short in their over-estimation of the physical. And, it is no doubt that humans fall prey in this way. When we are taught from childhood about an infinite physical universe—which is endless in all directions, it completely stifles spiritual thinking. When one imagines the physical as extending endlessly in all directions it poisons one's worldview.

But contrary to mainstream thinking, physical things are absolutely limited. They do not extend endlessly. And, once you understand that, you can for the first time step out of the physical dimensions which hold you captive.

The ground below a bird is limited and two-dimensional from his vantage. But by taking flight, the bird uses the third dimension of height to break free from the two-dimensions of the ground beneath. And, once the bird is above the ground, it is free of the dangers beneath.

Do you understand?

Just as a bird can break free of the two-dimensions of the ground beneath it, humans can break free of the physical dimensions which hold them physically captive. But whereas the bird breaks free through the dimension of height; humans break free through an unseen spiritual dimension—a 4th dimension. This is why humans are invited to walk by faith, not by sight. Although the bird is required to revisit the ground from time to time, he lives at will within the boundless skies above him. Likewise, although humans are required to attend to physical circumstances with their physical bodies, humans can live at will within the boundless spiritual world around them.

Did I just shatter your worldview?

Did I just break your over-estimation of the physical universe?

When understanding the true spiritual nature contained within our minds, we are capable of breaking free from the physical shackles around us.

101

As a human, you are not an animal. Although atheism wants to imprison you with that false thinking, you as a human are altogether different—being made in the image of God.

But I digress. If you enjoy reflecting on these thoughts, read my book, <u>Interview with the Time Traveler</u>.

Back to birds. . . .

Birds have wings. Those wings are what make them different from other creatures. Sure, some birds under the right circumstances can survive without flying. But, in the majority of cases, birds *need* to fly.

Without flight, birds are easy prey for ground predators. Without flight, many birds would have difficulty finding food. Even in the case of flightless birds, their wings are used for good purpose—thinking of penguins and ostriches for example. The penguin uses its wings while swimming and the ostrich uses its wings for posturing.

Question . . .

If we were to deny all birds the use of their wings, what changes would we see over the course of 100 years?

What birds would survive?

Sure, if a bird is protected it could continue to survive. But in the wild, many birds would die . . . very quickly in fact. Under the pressures exerted in the wild, birds who are denied their wings would quickly succumb to the regular austere conditions of the ground.

So, how does this relate to humans?

Atheistic naturalism works only in a world protected by police and militaries who have your best interests at heart. However, if that delicate bubble is broken, those "non-supernatural" humans would altogether lack the historic ability of humans to survive. Of course, if humans remain protected, living in ease and comfort, it could work for them to think of themselves as merely physical creatures.

But what happens when the merely physical human is exposed to unrelenting trauma?

I know what happens . . .

Either his mind finds a way to think "supernaturally"—that is beyond his physical circumstances—or it does not. He will either: (1) despair, or (2) find the will to live through anchoring his mind on a physically non-present reality.

Human history tells us only supernatural thinkers survive long-term. This is why supernatural thinking is ubiquitously associated with humanity. Those who cannot think supernaturally cannot find their will to live when they are pressed by trauma or hardship.

Period.

This is why all ancient humans all had beliefs in *something* spiritual.

In other words, when a person is plucked from their world of comfort and exposed to incredible tragedy, they tend to become spiritual. They either find a way to believe in *something* supernatural or they crumble from the inside-out. A non-physical thought or idea must become the mental anchoring point for the individual or they will be swept away with despair.

Keep in mind at this point I am not saying *what* they should choose to believe in—whether in invisible goblins or in an established religion. But my point is that all humans who encounter trauma *must* develop the ability to project their minds on supernatural thoughts of some kind.

Humans do this or they don't survive.

Period.

When considering naturalistic atheism, humans need to be wary. History provides us with data demonstrating humans do not survive long-term without supernatural beliefs. Unfortunately, by teaching humans to set aside spiritual beliefs, atheism may be contributing to the eventual destruction of humanity if ever it is plucked from the protected bubble of ease and comfort.

Therefore, when discussing ancient beliefs, do so with reverence—no matter how seemingly absurd. Don't scoff within your protected bubble at the "false beliefs" of ancient people—no matter how weird it may seem to consider beliefs in invisible goblins and such mystical things.

These ancient humans survived incredible trauma—which you likely cannot fathom. The development of ancient religions and mythology all hold within them profound supernatural ability. They helped people to survive the un-survivable.

However, in comparison, atheistic naturalism is a historically-inconsistent, ignorant snobbery. If ever atheism ventures to truly compete with any supernatural way of thinking or religion, the litmus test will be to determine if atheism can survive in an unprotected, brutal world long-term.

So far, it hasn't.

For example, let's discuss a religious system which is derided as false—Greek mythology. In all cases where it is discussed, Greek mythology is referred to as being false. (I don't know of anyone in the 21st Century who legitimately worships Zeus.)

But here is my point: From the perspective of human survival, Greek mythology is vastly superior to atheism.

"How?" you may ask.

Answer: Those people who believed in Greek mythology survived. And they developed a Hellenistic culture which transformed the entire world. By comparison, atheism has never proven itself as a sustainable system which can endure long-term.

Atheism has existed within the protected bubble provided by previous human generations. Although atheism takes a smug position against ancient religious humans, it is not even in the same league. The oft-derided Greek mythology system, although untrue, is nonetheless a time-tested, proven scaffolding capable of maintaining human societies long-term.

In this way, atheism is like a defiant child who ignorantly chides his own parents and grandparents who provided for his own upbringing. Atheism is brutal in its position against religion. Yet apart from religion, humanity itself would not exist. And by extension atheism would not exist.

So, in our example, even Greek mythology would appear as an aged, time-tested, experienced grandfather. But atheism would be like a defiant, untested child—altogether incapable of sustaining himself in the midst of a brutal world. In other words, atheism only exists when it is found within a protected system where the undisciplined can flourish. But when the defiant child is made to provide for himself, he quickly realizes the utility in the methods of his ancestors. The defiant child sets aside his critiques—struggling to remember for himself the methods taught to him in his childhood. If the child is intent on surviving, his best bet is to adopt the methods of those who learned to survive before him.

Here is an interesting thought . . .

Let's say you were planning to start a new country today. To ensure your country's long-term survival, you will need a plan. Within your planning process you will consider your country's ability to produce for its citizens, infrastructure, transportation, military and law.

When considering these different aspects of your new country, you will be ushered into the importance of religion as a means to pull the "big picture" together. Religion is indeed a proven, time-tested means of inspiring citizens. No matter how one may choose to disagree with religion, the contributions of religion to societies cannot be denied. Religion is the lynchpin of society survival. Without religion, the wheels fall off the carts of society!

So, what would be the religion of your country?

It is funny to consider, but your country would have a higher likelihood for long-term survival if you imported Greek mythology rather than atheistic naturalism!

At least mythology is a proven, time-tested means of inspiring humans. Whereas atheism is still a complete gamble for which there is no historical attestation for its long-term usefulness. In other words, telling humans they have no spirits is akin to telling birds they have no wings. So, atheism is indeed a most absurd denial of basic human nature and a major backward step in human "evolution."

Human history has already "selected" religious thinking for survival. Humans need supernatural thinking to survive long-term. So, why is atheism trying to "de-evolve" humanity?

Of course, there were many in ancient societies who altogether denied supernatural beliefs. But, just like the many extinct creatures of old, the brutality of the ancient world slowly dwindled those populations.

Until recent, spiritual thinking has been ubiquitously connected to humanity in every form—in every clime and place. No matter where we look in the ancient past, we encounter ancient people who all held spiritual beliefs. Yet, in the recent emergence of ease and comfort, protected by police and militaries, atheism has slowly awakened once again within humanity.

Atheism only works in a protected world of ease and comforts. When pressed, humans quickly revert to supernatural thinking—finding in those moments of testing that religion is a blessed means of respite.

Thus, the natural world itself provides a "natural selection" which works against human atheism. It is hilarious to think, and most ironic, that the principles of naturalism actually work against naturalism. In atheism, "survival of the fittest" is upheld. But when we look at ancient human history, we see only religious societies survived. Thus, religious humans are the most "fit" for survival—because all of human history demonstrates that form of human is the one most adept at survival.

Funny, right?

By upholding atheism, an atheist is denying the most "fit" form of humanity—the religious human. You just can't write this type of irony . . . er, uh, yeah, I guess I am writing it.

In conclusion, atheism arises in times of comfort, but in times of hardship it quickly ebbs. Thus, hardship provides a check against human atheism.

The natural form of surviving humanity is spiritual. Trauma always resets humans back to that original condition. Humans are spiritual by nature. A denial of human spirituality is as ridiculous as denying a bird his wings.

If you would like more information on the contributions of dissociation to the development of spiritual faith, read my book, <u>Dear David: Learning to See God through PTSD, Anxiety and Depression</u>. In this book I document the experiences of the ancient warrior, David, and his PTSD (post-traumatic stress disorder). Specifically, I explain how trauma leads to the development of spiritual thinking through "depersonalization" and "derealization."

Section III

Human Relationships & Religion

<u>8</u>:
The Natural Strength of Men & The Supernatural Power of Women

Consider a viper. A viper has no arms or legs, yet it can kill a lion with a single, darting strike.

In the ancient world, a viper would be (and was) seen to possess supernatural power. A viper is not naturally strong: It doesn't possess muscular strength that rivals other creatures. However, the viper's poison is mysteriously powerful—capable of subduing great beasts.

115

Similarly, in ancient human societies, men were inclined to view the "feminine" as divine. In fact, many ancient cultures revered goddesses.

Why?

To the brutish man, the power of the woman is exceptional and mysterious. A female human (in general) is physically weaker than a male human. Yet, somehow female humans possess great power apart from their lack of natural, physical strength.

After all, women possess the ability to subdue even the strongest men—as they inspire men to do their bidding. Moreover, women possess the ability to give birth to humans—a most miraculous ability.

Think about it . . .

A creature which lacks physical strength yet is able to accomplish great things is thought to possess "supernatural" power—that is power which is beyond mere natural power. Whereas a man may possess natural power in his muscles and ability to fight other men; a woman possesses "supernatural" power in her ability to subdue the strong man—persuading him to work for her. This is a supernatural ability by definition.

When considering humanity as a whole, it is no wonder why ancient humans would view the feminine as the true, spiritual form of humanity. The feminine is as enduring as the land—which holds fast under the endless passing of the sky above. From the feminine field, life springs forth miraculously.

But the male is as a hired tenant of the land. The female persuades the man of his lot—to work for her provisioning. Thus, in the ancient world, the male was most often relegated to the transient lot of a hired worker. He provides the seed for the field to propagate life, and he works all his days for the field.

Whereas many are inclined to view the Bible as a patriarchal system that oppresses women, this is not true. Rather, the Bible account of creation restored dignity to men in the midst of prevailing cultural views which compelled them to transience. The Bible encourages men to be fathers and husbands, rather than mere seed-donators.

So, the Genesis account of creation penned by Moses in the 15th Century B.C. challenged the concept of the pagan divine feminine. The account of creation occurred as it did for a reason . . . to remove from men the stigma of transience, seed-donation and work. Rather God sets forth His design in the creation account. Man is intended to join with woman as permanent members of a family. Thus, by returning dignity to men, the Bible account of creation establishes men and women as co-workers within their own families.

But I digress. Back to the topic . . .

For ancient humans, whenever they viewed a woman in a prominent social position it would have reinforced their thoughts of the supernatural. After all, a woman's prominence in the ancient world—whether as a ruler or a household manager—would show there was a supernatural law which superseded the natural world.

Ancient men were at first governed only by brute strength. And he who possessed the most physical strength and the strongest army was determined to be the head of all.

However, one woman could supplant this strong man. And without lifting a finger, the woman could find herself as the ruler of the strong man's entire household.

So, you must ask yourself . . .

Who was greater—the strong man with the best army, or the wife who subdued him?

Who held more power—the strong man or his wife?

Doubtlessly, the supernatural power of the wife was superior. During countless days, the strong man was left to endure life in the fields—with the heat of the day and the cold of each night afflicting him. The strong man was left to endure countless battlefields. Although wounded many times, the strong man continued to muster his strength to keep fighting—as a conscious recognition of the physical laws which govern men, ever struggling to remain atop challengers who sought to topple his headship.

However, as the strong man endured the discomforts of the field for countless days and nights, his wife remained within his stronghold. The strong man's physical proficiency purchased for his wife ever increasing safety from the common afflictions of the ancient world.

So, who was truly superior—the strong man or his wife?

Indeed, it is the wife.

From an outsider's perspective we see clearly the strong man was truly the servant of his wife. Without a doubt, the wife was greater than the strong man. From our neutral perspective, we can recognize the strong man as a mere worker-bee for his wife. He did all things to maintain his household, while his wife remained secure within his stronghold.

Therefore, in a most profound way, the mere presence of women teaches the reality of the "supernatural" to merely physical, brutish ancient men. Whereas women can effortlessly transcend all societal barriers through marriage, no such ladder of transcendence exists for men. Nor has it ever existed within the physical world: Physical men remain physical men.

In other words, a woman by marriage can immediately ascend all social barriers. But, on the other hand, men cannot. Or, to be more accurate, it just doesn't really happen.

Ask yourself, when was the last time you heard of a poor man marrying an extravagantly wealthy woman?

Funny, right?

Within this, we see the remarkable truth about humanity which was widely recognized by the ancients: The feminine is the eternal field which holds fast and from which miracles spring; but the masculine is relegated as a transient worker who is inwardly compelled to provide for the field. After all, seed is useless, unless it is planted.

Moreover, the supernatural power of the human feminine is so powerful it often achieves its purpose completely beyond perception. In a viper's strike of irony, the feminine convinces the male to do all things for her benefit, while paradoxically telling the male he is the head.

But, the reality of humanity stands. Humanity itself is governed by supernatural principles. This relationship of the natural-supernatural is an inherent part of the male-female existence of humanity.

So, I put forth the idea that humanity will never be capable of ridding itself of spirituality.

Why?

No matter how atheism may attempt to dismantle religious thinking, it will remain embedded within the female-male interaction of all humans. And, since the continuance of humanity requires the mingling of female and male in each generation to produce children, humans will never be capable of separating themselves from supernatural thinking.

When men view women in prominent positions, they are reminded of the supernatural law which supersedes all things in the natural world. The strongest men do not hold all the power. Rather, in a most paradoxical, supernatural fashion, power is held by those who lack natural strength.

Therefore, the cooperation of male and female in humanity demonstrates the supernatural. When brutish men view women, they receive glimpses of supernatural power.

A human can be "powerful" even if she is not "strong."

Cool, huh?

This is why all ancient human societies were religious. All societies had women. And when brutish men witnessed the transcendence achieved by noble women, they saw glimpses of supernatural power—which superseded mere physical strength.

So, as long as men can see women, men will be inclined to ponder the depths of supernatural power. Women, by their mere presence, move men to reflect upon supernatural principles. Therefore, as long as we are blessed with the presence of women, humanity will always be religious.

Always.

9:
Raising Children with "Tales"

We have heard it said, *"Children are our future."*

This is true.

We can be certain the raising of children was a central part of all successful ancient societies. Those societies which were the most adept at rearing children into productive citizens were the societies which flourished. But those societies which failed to effectively raise children were incapable of long-term survival.

123

So, how does this concept intersect with the discussion of religion?

Consider this . . .

Have you ever wondered why children are so inclined to believe in supernatural things?

Think about it . . .

Children are often intrigued and captivated by thoughts of mythical animals and creatures. They watch cartoons which are colorful, lively and otherworldly. Children tend to enjoy magic and just about anything which combines the supernatural with the physical.

Why?

The answer is *very* easy: Throughout human history, the children who were the most inclined to believe in spiritual things were the ones who survived! But children who were not inclined to believe in superstitious tales did not survive. And, when you multiply this effect over the course of countless generations, we see the product . . . human children are now overwhelmingly open to spiritual things.

Interesting, huh? Re-read that if you must. Allow it to sink in.

Whereas an adult may scoff at a ghost story, children will readily accept it—and immediately modify their behavior. If a child is told a convincing story about a haunted house, he will accept the story and re-tell it to others. And that story will modify his behavior—whether it inspires him to only go near the house in a group or to stay away from it altogether. But the fact remains— human children are inclined to believe in spiritual things.

So, let's examine how religion was used to ensure child survival and societal integration . . .

Superstitions are one of the most effective methods of raising children. Historically this is proven— as attested by the success of ancient religious societies. When children are raised with religious values and superstitions, they are most likely to develop into adults who are well-adapted to the values of their societies.

Of course, those who are critical of religion may voice ethical considerations on whether it is proper to use superstitions in parenting techniques.

Granted.

However, one cannot debate the effectiveness of superstitions in influencing the behavior of children. In the comfortable, mamby pamby 21st Century, people can sneer at ancients—scoffing their use of superstitions to stop their children from doing certain things.

But we must remember in the ancient world "death" was an ever-present threat, and not every child survived.

So, if you were an ancient parent, you would do everything you could to increase your child's odds of surviving common dangers—to the point of using superstitious tales of goblins, ghosts or whatever to influence them to conform to the rules of your society and household.

Remember, in the ancient world, either children learned quickly or they died.

Therefore, survival of families and the clan depended on the use of the most effective parenting techniques. And, as it turns out, "religion" was the most effective means of training children in the ancient world. This is evidenced by the fact that all ancient human societies were religious—which means all those societies obviously used their religion to good effect for many successive generations as a part of their culture.

Neat, huh?

Let's explore a scenario . . .

Imagine you are an ancient mother who is raising a young child. At this stage in his life you are beginning to teach your child to do certain household chores—feeding animals, cleaning and other tasks. In your parenting techniques, there are two different approaches you could take . . .

First, you could simply tell your son which chores he is assigned, then supervise him in accomplishing his chores. But as we all know, over time he will likely lose his motivation. From time to time he may forget tasks—and doubtlessly you will need to provide continued guidance to help him incorporate the chores into his daily routine.

Or, second, you could use a "superstitious tale" to influence your son's behavior. This is an even more effective approach—which was used often by our ancient ancestors.

As we discussed, children are biologically inclined to believe in spiritual things. They are ingrained with the desire to believe in supernatural things. Thus, an ancient parent who used "stories" in their parenting became more effective at influencing lasting behavioral change.

In ancient Europe, families would do this by teaching their children about *household goblins*. It was common for parents to refer to the household goblins as creatures who were kind, but easily agitated when those in the family did certain negative things. This was a remarkable means of parenting.

Why?

Well, children are biologically wired to believe in spiritual things. They enjoy hearing stories and tales—especially when they are included within them. So, the idea of quiet, helpful household goblins which watched over the family as they slept was a comforting thought.

Moreover, the more convincing the stories told by the parents, the more effective they became at influencing the child's behavior.

For example, the parent could leave out a cookie overnight, then in the morning show the child nibble marks on the cookie—telling of the goblin eating his nightly meal. The parent could move various things in the house—telling the child it was done by the goblin. Also, if the parent let the child name the household goblin, this might make the child feel an emotional connection to the story.

As the parent added to the tale of the household goblin, it became much more convincing, and therefore much more capable of influencing the child. Therefore, the tale of a household goblin was one which could continue to be embellished—thereby gaining additional buy-in from the child.

In cases where the child misbehaved or was negligent of his duties, the parent could simply appeal to the household goblin—telling the child his behavior was going to make the household goblin angry.

And this is where this method becomes very interesting . . .

Whereas a child might be inclined to misbehave for his mother; a child would *not* be inclined to continue that behavior if told it offended the household goblin.

Why?

Because there is no "point of reference" for a goblin. The child has never seen a goblin—so the child is left to wonder perilously at what tragedy *might* occur if he were to anger a goblin. The child is left to wonder at the extent of the goblin's power and ferocity—being incapable of imagining what the goblin *might* be capable of. And, within this mystery of the superstitious tale, the child becomes self-persuaded to abandon his misbehavior.

However, the child will disrespect his mother, because the child knows how quickly her anger subsides and is replaced with compassion. But to anger a goblin— that is a most foolish venture for a child who truly "believes" in the household goblin.

In this way, ancient humans used superstitious tales like these to influence the behavior of their children. The household goblin tale could take shape within the family as it would be further embellished by the parents. And over time, the child would own the tale as a part of his childhood—in turn teaching it to his own children.

Although those who are critical of religion may bemoan this method, it is very effective and most entertaining. Throughout all human history, this type of method was the one used by successful human societies.

Moreover, its entertainment factor is priceless— especially when placed within a dull, ancient world. It is fun to think about a mother sharing a tale with her son, as they both add to it throughout their blessed years together. The whole point was that the mother took an interest in her child, loving him enough to do everything in her power to persuade him to become a responsible young adult. In this, it is most beautiful and heart-warming.

Sure, a parent could use an "atheist" method of teaching the child to do chores—simply stating the task and supervising its completion. But what is the fun in that? . . . *Super boring!*

At least by talking about a household goblin and allowing the tale to take form over time, it provided a silly, albeit serious, means through which the mother could regularly interact with her child.

Children love imaginative stories, and superstitious tales deliver. This is why the superstitious societies were the most effective at raising successive generations of children. Their superstitious tales were captivating and inspiring—capable of producing acceptable behavior in children.

Inherent within this method, it is understood that eventually the adolescent child would have realized there was no household goblin—much as a child today might figure out Santa Claus doesn't exist. But that's not the point. The point is the value of the story in influencing behavior—and in that it is subjectively useful. The objective facts don't matter.

And, just as every good mother desires to bless her child in miraculous ways, a shared superstitious tale was the mother's attempt to bless her son with otherworldly magic—if only for a moment. After all, an ancient child would be left to endure sufficient physical tragedy throughout his entire lifetime—long after the loss of his mother. So, what is the harm in him believing in a friendly household goblin while he was young—coaching him in the development of personal responsibility in preparation for adulthood?

131

Thus, although the adolescent child came to the realization that the story was merely a story, he came to value it nonetheless—thinking upon it fondly and the laughs he shared with his mother as they discussed nibbled cookies.

What's wrong with that?

With this thought, the adolescent child would resolve to teach the same story to his own child someday—using it to influence him to develop responsibility. And, perhaps within this choice to continue the myth, the now deceased mother achieved her purpose in blessing her son with the miraculous. Apart from her superstitious tale, her son would have perished in his childhood. But the miracle was achieved by her tale of the "household goblin." . . . Her son survived! He overcame all the dangers of the ancient world which confronted him in his childhood. And the tale helped him to remain true to the rules taught to him by his mother. . . . And after the son survived, another miracle occurred as his own children also survived through the use of the same superstitious tale of the household goblin.

In the grandest estimation, there is no greater miracle than saving life which would otherwise have been lost. And, in this way, even the most seemingly absurd tales were blessings to the families in which they were told. Any tale which saved the life of children in the ancient world was by definition "miraculous."

From time immemorable, this was the pattern within all ancient human societies. Children were raised by the use of myths—some silly, some serious, but always inspirational and capable of influencing them in the development of acceptable social values. That is the point.

Have you ever wondered why children don't seem like they mind their parents anymore? This is why. Humans no longer use the parenting methods which were regularly employed throughout all of human history.

Understand a child's inclination toward spiritual things. Then relate to the child in those terms—telling silly stories which inspire them.

Or, to say this another way . . .

Humans in the 21st Century have forgotten what it means to "be human." Look to the history of humanity and the conditions under which it thrived—then find ways to return to those basic principles which allowed humans in the past to flourish. Don't shy away from your humanity, but embrace it.

Allow children to be spiritual.

Teach them to believe.

Teach them to "see" with their hearts (2 Cor. 5:7).

Abandon the dull, merely physical methods of atheism. Atheism never produced successful societies—and it won't start now.

If you want to know how to effectively raise children, begin by studying the methods of religions which have produced the most enduring human societies. Avoid 21st Century parenting techniques taught by atheists. They are ineffective and boring. Rather, be an interesting, spiritual, miracle-producing parent. Make fun stories with your child. Cherish the time you have with your child.

Section IV

Community Development
&
Religion

<u>10</u>:
Ancient City Development & The Vital Contribution of Religion

For me, "city development" is an interesting topic. When viewing some of the most magnificent ancient cities, we are left to wonder how they achieved such success—especially when many ancient cities did not.

So, in this chapter we will discuss how and why ancient humans formed cities. I trust this chapter will present many interesting things for your consideration.

Begin by imagining ancient humans existing in small family groups. Within these small family groups, individuals supported one another.

But, for a city to emerge, it takes much more than a single-family group.

So, what originally compelled single-family groups to form cities?

And, how did those small family groups become large communities?

As you read further, I will explain how this occurred. As a whole, city development involves **nine steps** . . .

#1 Uniting Family Groups

The **first step** in ancient city development is "uniting family groups." The small family groups must unite—most likely through intermarriage with one another.

#2 Calorie Limit

The **second step** in ancient city development is "calorie limit." The combined family groups must have sufficient food to provide for all humans and livestock within their growing city community. And, in the ancient world, this could be challenging.

This raises logistical concerns because the location of the growing group must be situated where there is ample water and land available to grow necessary crops.

Although this may be difficult to comprehend, picture it this way: If you have a group of 100 people, those 100 people require a certain number of calories every day. So, let's say each person on average requires 1500 calories each day. This means the land and water on which you are situated must be capable of providing 1500 calories multiplied by 100 people every day. This totals 150,000 calories. Over the course of one year, your group of 100 humans will need to obtain 54,750,000 calories from their land and water source just to sustain themselves.

Calculating how these calories are obtained may be somewhat complicated when we consider the various food sources. For example, the 100 people could fish, hunt, gather and use agriculture.

But, what if this group of 100 humans failed to obtain the required calories they needed to survive?

The answer is simple: They disperse.

Throughout history, whenever a group of humans failed to obtain the required calories in a specific location, they moved away from one another.

When understanding this basic fact about humans, the development of "cities" is remarkable. Ancient cities were always at risk of being dispersed. If people failed to receive adequate calories they would immediately begin to think about dispersing.

(Remember, there is safety within numbers—so, as an ancient city leader, you have a personal interest in keeping your city's population as numerous as possible. If your people disperse this will make you and your family "sitting ducks" for other larger groups intent on your destruction.)

So, if you were an ancient city leader, what would be the most dependable method for you to ensure your people were provided for—in order to stop people from dispersing?

Of course, the most dependable source of calories would be agriculture.

If the 100 humans knew how to dry and store grain, perhaps they could obtain the required 54,750,000 calories annually just by harvesting their grain. In this way agriculture provided ancient cities with the means of sustenance when they couldn't hunt, fish or gather.

However, agriculture presents problems as a group grows larger. Sure, land can provide crops and a group may know how to preserve those crops for year-round use. But, as the group grows, the amount of land needed to grow crops likewise increases. Eventually, the amount of farmland needed to produce the required calories to support all the people becomes very great. This leads us to the third step in ancient city development . . .

#3 Transportation

The **third step** in ancient city development is "transportation."

At this stage in ancient city development, the amount of land needed to support a city with a high population becomes so large that crops can no longer be moved into the city by foot. The farmland becomes so dispersed—so far beyond the city walls—the people must build roads and carts to transport their grain.

So, as a city grows, if at any point they fail in their ability to provide an effective means of "transportation," the city may collapse and the people disperse into the countryside.

At the beginning, roads were little more than trails made by farmers in an attempt to help them to move their own crops. Assuming an ancient city was successful at linking these trails into a roadway system, the city could continue to grow—perhaps to a population exceeding 1,000 people.

Waterways also provide a helpful means of transportation. Cities situated on rivers, lakes or streams could use boats to transport crops from faraway farmlands into the city limits.

But regardless of the means of transport, the fact remains: An ancient city's growth was directly determined by logistics. If the city leader was creative enough to develop effective methods of transportation, then his city would continue to grow. But if at any time his transportation network failed to bring the required calories to the people in the city, his city would rapidly disperse into the surrounding countryside.

#4 Military

The **fourth step** in ancient city development is "military." To grow further, the city would require the use of more farmland, even further from its previous farmland, just to provide the required minimum calories to its citizens. To do this, the city is no longer concerned with *just* roads and carts. Now the city becomes concerned with "security."

As crops are transported from the far-off farmlands to the city, farmers may be threatened by bandits on the country roads. So, the city leader would need an army to patrol its farmland roads and waterways. This city military would fight bandits, allowing citizens to continue in their normal roadway activities—transporting their crops into the city.

Beyond this, the use of security forces provides additional enhancements to the city. As the security forces fought bandits, they became transformed in purpose. The city's military no longer just patrolled roads. Rather they began to seek out threats in the vast countryside *before* they could emerge. Thus, the security forces became an army—carrying out military operations in pursuit of their city's best interests.

As a city grew, it would always need more farmland. The city needed more farmland to produce additional crops for the growing population.

So, how did an ancient city get more farmland?

You guessed it . . . their military fought for it.

Therefore, the security forces of an ancient city not only provided for security on roadways, but they actively sought ways to conquer new lands. So, the city leader would constantly be aware of what was happening in the lands adjacent to his city's farmlands. And, if opportunity presented itself, the city leader would order his army to attack and seize more farmland.

In this way, the introduction of the military to ancient cities compelled adjacent cities to grow. Competing cities were ever wary of one another. And, if at any time, a city began to wane in its numbers compared to adjacent cities, those adjacent cities would begin considering how they could use their military to seize their farmlands.

This is a simple concept which was in the best interest of all ancient cities. More farmland meant more crops. And more crops meant the city could support a larger population. Which, in turn, meant the city could support a larger military. Then, as a city grew its military, it further grew its ability to fight and gain more farmland. Then the process repeats.

Cool, right?

This is why it is always funny to hear 21ˢᵗ Century people bemoan their country's defense budget—wrongly assuming money is "wasted" when it is allocated to national defense. But history tells us that military power is the time-tested means to achieving national interests. Thus, for powerful nations, a powerful military gives a nation the ability to readily form allies. And in this way the military can be used by wise leaders to gain strategic advantages and bolster their economy on the world stage.

It is interesting to consider how militaries have always been critical components of human societies. Successful cities, whether in antiquity or the present, have always needed military forces to achieve their national interests. But societies which objected to militaries were eventually defeated by militaries.

#5 Government

The **fifth step** in ancient city development is "government." Along with the need for a military, a <u>fifth</u> requirement arises: "government." A military which patrols the roadways needs a leadership structure to govern it. The military of an ancient city was a vital component contributing to its growth—perhaps even the most important. Therefore, officers appointed as leaders in the city's military bore special commissioning from the highest city leader. As these military officers were sent out from the city, they went with the highest endorsement of the city leader—ordered to carry out his will in far-off lands.

Remarkably, today in the 21st Century, it is still common for even the lowest ranking officers and leaders in the military to have their commissions come directly from the president of an entire country.

Why?

Because the success of ancient cities was dependent upon its military. If the military was proficient, the city would grow. But if the military lacked proficiency, the city would wane—eventually becoming liable to destruction from competing adjacent cities.

This is why it is in the best interest of all cities and countries to "support their troops." If any gathering of humans fails to provide for its security with diligence, it will eventually be overtaken by another competing group.

So, on the most foundational level, the most important purpose of human government is to establish and maintain its military. This is why ancient kings were also great military leaders. In fact, if a military was powerful enough, it could even intimidate adjacent groups so thoroughly that they agreed to make large payments just to avoid battle. Moreover, smaller cities would swear allegiance to larger ones, paying tribute to cities with the largest armies for the privilege of falling under their protection.

Frankly, many of these concepts are beyond the grasp of sheltered readers in the 21st Century. But you must recognize the default operation of the world is based upon physical brutality and military force. This is why pampered people in the 21st Century do not understand ancient people. They do not understand what it was like to live in a brutal ancient world where there was no escape from trauma.

But if you carefully read and understand what I am saying, then the function of religion will make perfect sense. The spirituality of humanity was, and is, their only hope.

In addition to overseeing the military, the rudimentary city government might at its earlier stages work to link together the small roadways of various farms—thereby providing more effective means to move its military throughout its kingdom.

#6 Taxes

The **sixth step** in ancient city development is "taxes." In order to provide for the army and its oversight, the government levies "taxes." Simply put, in the ancient world, a city's ability to defend itself was the only way it could continue to exist. Without a well-trained, proficient military, a city and its farmlands would be quickly seized by another competing city with a better army. So, in its basic form, taxes were originally intended to provide for the continued security of cities. Soldiers who gave their full attention to patrolling were paid from the abundance of the city.

Remember the basic calorie requirements of the city upon which its continued existence relies?

A city can employ a military, but it must do so with balance. The soldiers give their full attention to patrolling and as such must be paid by the crops of the farmers they protect. But to determine the number of soldiers a city can reasonably employ, a government official must determine the excess "calories" of the city. The amount of food excess will tell the government official how many soldiers he can employ.

Thus, the employment of more soldiers either accelerates or restricts the growth of the city. If the government employs more soldiers, this allows them to gain more farmland and hold it securely. But, if at any time the city wanes in its ability to provide well-trained soldiers in its far-off countryside, other competing cities may seize its land. In this way, a well-equipped, well-trained, numerous army is perhaps the most decisive city growth factor.

#7 Law

The **seventh step** in ancient city development is "law." Within the ancient city, "law" was needed to govern the behavior of citizens within the city and also farming families in the surrounding countryside.

The city leader would set the rules. And, in the establishment of his rules, the city leader must have ability to enforce those rules—which leads to the next step in ancient city development . . .

#8 Law Enforcement

The **eighth step** in ancient city development is "law enforcement." The established military, originally intended to patrol roadways and fight for territories, now assumes the additional responsibility of providing "law enforcement" amongst citizens.

But this presents a logistical problem. Frankly, the city's military is never large enough to police *all* its far-off territories. Although "enforcing laws" within city limits is feasible; enforcing laws in the vastly dispersed farmlands and countryside are a near impossibility. Thus, the city leader needs some other means of law enforcement to control his vast farmland territories. This brings us to our next step in ancient city development . . .

#9 Religion

Last of all, "religion" finds its place as the supernatural assistant to all these steps in city development.

How?

Well, religion provides a means to cover gaps in these above eight steps. Specifically, religion is the means through which the city leader can indirectly influence the behavior of his citizens in far-off farmland settlements.

Sure, a city leader could travel with his military force to various farming hamlets. But it is not feasible for the city leader to provide for justice in all these vast regions. So, the countryside people must be governed by an ethereal "law"—one which needs minimal enforcement.

And, as it turns out, religion is the best fulfillment of this requirement. Religion has great purpose is governing the hearts of citizens—helping them to be a "law" unto themselves.

So, how would a city leader incorporate religion into his city development plan?

Simple . . . The city leader and his officials propagate inspiring supernatural tales which exemplify the desired behavior for citizens. For example, if a city leader needed a stronger army, then the best way to influence the army's development would be to propagate inspiring tales about heroes and valor. These superstitious tales would infuse the vast countryside—inspiring young men to grow into warriors like the heroes in the supernatural tales.

In all ways, religion is a superb addition to human society. Religion trumps steps similar to how "trade" trumps steps.

For example, if a city were to develop the ability to create prized items, it could trade its items for food. So, rather than focusing on providing its own agriculture, a trading city may simply barter for it. Thus, trade allows a city to go around certain steps.

But, unlike trading—which is only beneficial at certain points for a city; religion is the ultimate enhancing factor for a city.

How?

Let's examine how religion, or superstitious beliefs, help city development in all the above listed steps . . .

Family Groups are United by Religion

In step #1 of city development, we saw small family groups must unite to form a city. Of course, intermarriage among members in different groups is a way this is accomplished.

But in order to make vows of marriage, it is common to appeal to a higher, spiritual power. In ungoverned lands which precede the development of cities, it is necessary for rival family groups to hold one another accountable. And, the best way to do this is through appealing to the unseen, supernatural forces which are believed to hold together the physical world.

Thus, religion becomes a central means through which groups unite.

This is especially true in the case of two rival groups whose physical strength is equal. Both family groups would be incapable of winning against its counterpart in battle. Therefore, the swearing of religious oaths provides a means to hold one another accountable without suffering loss. And in this way, religion provides for self-preservation of mutual groups. In other words, the people can trust the supernatural beings to look out for their best interests—thereby assuaging their desire to fight rival groups. Thus, religious oaths provide a rational means through which competing groups can unite with one another; whereas without religion, the two groups would remain brutish competitors.

Neat, huh?

When groups choose to "swear allegiance" to one another, they must have a means to hold one another accountable. By swearing in the name of unseen spiritual powers, the rival groups become capable of showing integrity. In the midst of ungoverned lands, religious oaths which appeal to the spiritual world are the most common means of holding one another accountable.

In other words, if a rival group leader goes back on his word, then spiritual powers were believed to be responsible for punishing him—even if his family group was stronger than the family group he offended.

Thus, religion provides a means of justice to smaller groups in the midst of an otherwise brutal ancient world. Apart from religious oaths, the powerful were free to do whatever they desired. However, when ancient humans truly believed in their religions, those religions set boundaries for their behavior.

For the first time, when brutish men began to believe in the supernatural, they began to feel "guilt" and "shame" when they wronged their fellow man. And, the more one believed in his religion, the more his religion influenced his behavior—providing for himself an inward system of positive-reinforcement and negative-reinforcement.

This was the power in ancient religion. It helped brutish men find their way to decent behavior—albeit still violent, but perhaps far less violent than it would have been otherwise. And, for the first time, less powerful family groups finally had a foothold upon which they could advance among other competing groups. The beliefs of the strongest family group leaders pacified them—encouraging them to be charitable to smaller family groups, rather than fighting them.

So, in all cases in the ancient world, when dealing with the leader of a powerful rival group, your best bet would be to require your rival to take an oath in the name of his own gods—in whom he believed. Frankly, this would have been your only hope. Although the rival leader may have been tempted to later betray his promise to you, his oath—and the fear of his gods—would have compelled him to remain true.

Do you see why religion is so important to human development?

Furthermore, "founding myths" have always been used to unite groups of people. In Greek city-states this was common, as each city-state developed a myth which explained how their city was discovered or established through the actions of gods or goddesses. In these cases, the development of a "founding myth" gave each city-state a standing among rival city-states.

Additionally, "founding myths" rallied a city's people to stay true to their city as a reflection of their allegiance to the divine powers which were said to have led to its discovery. Whereas an ancient human may have been tempted to desert their city leader; an ancient human would be far less inclined to desert a city which he believed was founded by his god.

So, religion was most effective at uniting family groups. Religion kept rival group leaders faithful to their promises. Religion made the most powerful leaders more capable of mercy by giving them a devout fear of divine punishment. And, once religion united family groups, it kept them faithful to one another.

Religion Staves off Calorie Limit Dispersion

When considering religion, why do you suppose "self-denial" is often held in high esteem? Why is "fasting" a regular practice of many religions?

Answer: Religious practices, like self-denial and fasting, push individuals to stay committed despite temporary set-backs.

Why is this important?

Earlier we discussed the "calorie limit" of a growing city—where a group of people would be required to find enough food to meet the basic calorie requirements of its people. Whenever a growing city became incapable of providing enough calories for its people, their bond would be broken and they would disperse.

Indeed, when viewing the archeological remains of ancient societies, we find many cities which likely crumbled during brief food shortages. Truly, ancient cities were vulnerable as people are ever inclined to disperse whenever they are pressed by hardship.

However, through the use of spiritual beliefs, and the upholding of practices, such as fasting and self-denial, religion provides the means to hold people together longer—even in the midst of shortages.

Indeed, these practices did not emerge by chance. Rather, fasting and self-denial as parts of religious practice are incredibly useful. In fact, we could say the discipline achieved by these religious practices directly contributed to the success of ancient religious cities. In other words, the city which fasted together stayed together.

When religion teaches individuals self-discipline it enables adherents to develop the inner discipline to "stay the course" longer during hardship. If in times of abundance citizens are encouraged to fast as a part of their worship, this means they will possess the inner discipline to stay true to themselves and others when there is an actual food shortage.

Cool, right?

In other words, over time the cities which survived were the ones which consisted of the most superstitious citizens who were practiced in self-denial. But, the cities in which self-denial was not upheld as a religious virtue were doomed to eventual dispersion. In this way, superstitious beliefs and its requisite self-denial allowed cities to push past difficult times while remaining united to one another.

But non-religious individuals would have possessed no self-discipline to allow them to stay true to their city in times of hardship. Whereas a self-denying religious person would be accustomed to a healthy self-affliction; a non-religious person would have been governed by his belly—compelled to flee into the countryside.

This is why all ancient human societies were religious. The religious citizens stayed true through their self-discipline; but the non-religious citizens slithered away. Through successive periods of hardship, ancient cities ever decreased the amount of non-religious citizens within because they lacked the self-discipline to endure.

Transportation & Superstitions

Superstitions contributed to the safety of religious people as they travelled roads. Later in this book I will discuss the myth of the "darting wraith" in detail on pages 248-253. In that discussion I explain that those who believed in superstitions were the *most likely* to avoid common dangers. And, over time, this meant more superstitious humans survived than non-superstitious humans. In turn, this is why all ancient human societies were religious: Only the superstitious people survived.

My myth of the "darting wraith" illustrates the vast usefulness of myths to ancient people. In the case of the darting wraith myth, ancient humans would have held a healthy wariness of the dangers present in the world around them.

For example, a man who sincerely believed in wilderness wraiths would have been less inclined to venture off the roads—thereby reducing his chances of getting lost or hypothermia. Moreover, a man who believed in wilderness wraiths would have been more wary of other people he met on the road—suspecting them of being wraiths in disguise. Thus, the superstitious man would have been much more likely to evade harassment from bandits.

Furthermore, superstitions provided a healthy self-assurance for travelers. By believing in spiritual beings who help people during their travels, the believer automatically benefits from the placebo effect and confirmation bias. Whether one's beliefs are validated by a skeptic is irrelevant. Whereas atheism may assert the superstitious beliefs of our ancient ancestors were wrong, it is undeniable their sincerely held beliefs produced within them a helpful psychological effect—boosting their confidence and giving them the ability to press ahead despite difficulties.

Concerning "transportation," it is also interesting to consider how religion may have granted ancient humans the supernatural means to move massive objects.

For example, many ancient monuments were built using incredibly heavy rocks. To many it is an absolute mystery.

How indeed were ancient humans capable of moving such heavy objects?

From a 21st Century perspective, there is much of the ancient world which escapes understanding. Perhaps in your estimation you might conclude that religion at times provided humans with the ability to do the otherwise impossible. Ancient monuments seem to demonstrate this fact.

So, why were all ancient societies religious?

The answer might be very simple . . .

Ancient humans might have routinely witnessed displays of actual supernatural power. Indeed, it is interesting to consider. As you look further into the ancient past of humanity, make sure you look at ancient monuments. Reflect on the possibility that religion may hold within itself the power to do the physically impossible. Perhaps that is the timeless message conveyed to us by all ancient monuments. Decide for yourself.

Security & Superstitions

Superstitious people are less likely to be victims. The more one believes in superstitions, the less likely he will be taken by surprise. Thus, from a security perspective, superstitious people would be more vigilant and aware of their surroundings. This means they would be more inclined to escape danger—whether from predators, bandits or environmental conditions.

And since the superstitions of the superstitious man protect him from danger, he is better suited to thrive in the far-off country lands outside the protection of the city's walls. Whereas the non-superstitious man relies upon police protection to safeguard him against danger; the superstitious man's extreme vigilance is sufficient for his protection. This means that when an ancient city would struggle to provide for its army, superstitious people were more likely to continue to thrive in far-off farmlands than their non-superstitious counterparts.

Superstitious people would have a healthy wariness of the roads they travelled. For example, a man who believed in wilderness wraiths would be more wary of fellow travelers he met on the road, supposing they may be wraiths in disguise. At times this wariness of fellow travelers may have saved the religious man from bandit attacks.

By holding superstitions, country farmers become somewhat capable of providing for their own security. The first step toward security is to make yourself a "hard target"—one that is more resistant to bandit attack.

Superstitions can be added to myths to provide additional security for believers. For example, if using my "darting wraith" myth, a group of farmers may choose to re-tell the myth with different details as they sit around a campfire. They may say to one another that the darting wraith is attracted to shiny objects. So, in this way, the repeated telling of this additional detail in the myth would have dissuaded believers from leaving shiny objects uncovered during their travels. This myth addition would make these superstitious farmers even harder targets because they would take additional measures to conceal all valuable "shiny" items.

The myth could also be modified to say the darting wraith is scared by companies of ten or more people. As the myth is re-told with this detail, those who believe in it would be encouraged to travel only at times when other farmers were also travelling. This would make them even harder targets for bandits because the myth would encourage all the superstitious farmers to travel in large caravan groups, rather than travelling alone.

Therefore, over time, those who believed in religious myths would become increasingly more secure on the roads through their superstitious beliefs.

So, why were all ancient societies religious?

Because superstitions provide an interesting means through which individuals benefit from the lessons of others. Stories are memorable. Thus, they are perhaps the best means of influencing behavior change. Religion takes advantage of stories to inspire and help people. Therefore, the most superstitious people were the most likely to survive common threats.

In other words, superstitious people thrive better than non-superstitious people in the absence of a police force. Superstitious people intentionally embellish tales, adding helpful details, to help one another to be vigilant and prepared against likely threats. But non-superstitious people foolishly disregarded this most effective method of corporate behavior adjustment through storytelling. And, as a result, the non-superstitious people were more likely to perish from various threats in the countryside— whether predator, bandit or environmental conditions.

In other words, history proves atheism only works in a world where the non-religious are protected by a police force and military. But whenever that delicate protective bubble is popped, people do not thrive apart from the vigilance provided by superstitious thinking.

This is why all ancient societies were religious. The most superstitious humans were best suited for survival. Superstitious people guarded themselves against danger by learning from one another and adopting heartfelt spiritual beliefs which saved their lives.

Government & Superstitions

In the above discussion of "government," we explained government's responsibility for administering the city's military.

Even though superstitions do not directly rule government, in many cases religious leaders serve as administrators. Indeed, when considering how superstitions possess within themselves the ability to influence the behavior of citizens and to provide for subtle changes in society for its benefit, religious leaders would be seen as having their hands upon the pulse of the people. Thus, religious leaders would possess the greatest psychological understanding of common citizens and be in the best position to indirectly move the people using their ethereal, veiled ability.

Of course, within the ancient context, I am not referring to "official" religious leaders. Rather, the "religious leaders" within ancient societies might be best understood at those who were the most skilled at speaking inspiring tales. Those who could best influence the hearts of others would be the ones capable of gaining followings.

When holding this basic understanding of religion, we quickly recognize that this influence is not granted as a part of an "officially-recognized" appointment. Rather, ancient religious leaders were the ones who were the most inspirational speakers. And, their effectiveness was assessed by whether or not they produced lasting, beneficial change within their group or city.

Indeed, the basis for human government is founded within religion. Whereas the non-religious person believes himself beholden to no power beyond himself, being convinced otherwise only by brute, physical force; the religious person readily acknowledges the right to rule as an extension of divine power.

By supposing an ethereal, supernatural power which governs the physical world, ancient humans established the right of human government to rule over citizens. This is how it worked . . .

The ancient religious person reasoned, "Since spiritual powers require no consent for their rulership of Earth, nor do human leaders require consent from those they govern." And, upon this religious foundation, the establishment of government is firmly placed.

Although one may be inclined to view superstitious humans as naïve consenters to government rule, we must remind ourselves that religion was the only real pathway to survival in the ancient world. As such, in order for humanity to advance, humanity required individuals to submit to one another. Those non-religious humans who consented to no power beyond themselves were slowly dissipated by larger, powerful societies of superstitious people who did choose to unite—even if it meant their personal abasement.

After all, when one is religious, his abasement in the physical world is not even viewed as an abasement. Those who are superstitious can hold the belief that the physical world is only a shadow of the true spiritual world. Thus, the religious person values spiritual advancement rather than worldly advancement. This means the religious man has power to relegate the entire physical world, and all its troubles, to a scoffing dismissal. Thus, superstitious belief lends to the establishment of government. Those who are religious consent to being governed—which in turn increases their likelihood for mass survival.

This is why all ancient human societies were religious. Belief in *supernatural* government without consent leads to the rational establishment of *human* government without consent. And, those who are religious are more inclined to submit to government leadership as model citizens—enduring hardship through the disciplines they gain in religious devotion, ultimately setting aside the pleasures of this physical world in preference for the afterlife.

This is why all ancient human societies were religious.

Cool, right?

Taxes & Superstitions

As discussed above, religions often uphold "self-denial" as virtuous. Earlier we discussed how fasting as a practice hardens citizens in preparation for set-backs. Likewise, religion in its self-denial often upholds alms-giving as a regular practice.

Therefore, it is obvious why religious cities, consisting of religious people, were more likely to survive. Those who have incorporated into their regular behavior the practices of "giving" are more likely to give what they must for the defense and maintenance of their city.

Thus, ancient cities which were religious were more likely to have soldiers. And if they needed to scrimp to provide for their city, ancient religious people were already accustomed to fasting. So, if they needed to go without food for a couple days to provide for their city, they would be able and willing to do so.

Moreover, if religious people believed their city to be founded by the god or goddess whom they worshipped, they would be willing to give to the uttermost for its defense. Clearly, this is why all ancient human societies were religious. The fervor they felt for their people was continually fueled by their heartfelt beliefs. And, they were disciplined—practiced in the useful methods of fasting and alms giving.

In other words, an atheist could walk away from a city; but the firmly held beliefs of the religious man compelled him to give all to maintain his city. Therefore, all ancient human societies were religious. The beliefs of the devout man compelled him to stay, and his religious virtues gave him the discipline to endure.

Atheism possesses no such endurance.

Law & Superstitions

A government can publish laws, but they bear little weight with countryside citizens who are out of the reach of law enforcement.

Within the city itself, laws can be enforced. However, in the vast countryside—where no police are present, being seen only as they patrol the roadways—the city's government is altogether incapable of overseeing the behavior of citizens.

Sure, when a dissenter is found by police, they can punish him brutally in an attempt to dissuade his countrymen from similar behavior. But, these rare instances of punishment are altogether insufficient—even if tales of them reach the ears of people in these outlying farmlands.

And, even more remarkable, when a man is desperate, he will do things without concern for law. This always surprises people, but when a man has nothing to live for, with no incentive for greatness and no dream beyond his current condition, he throws off restraint and does whatever he desires—being unconcerned with whether or not he is caught. After all, he is convinced he has nothing to live for. He just takes whatever he wants and operates in the shadows. This man does not care about legal definitions. He doesn't care what the law determines to be called "murder," "rape," "theft," or any such distinctions. He simply doesn't care. He throws off all restraint.

Once you understand the desperate condition which afflicts many humans, you can open your eyes to see the vital contribution of religion. Indeed, religion is the "only" means to govern the truly desperate man who lives beyond the reach of law enforcement. The only hope for reformation for the desperate man is to change his heart from within through religion.

Religion is the "only hope" of a city government to influence countryside behavior. Soldiers and police are limited, but religion is ubiquitous. Religion teaches the omnipresence of spiritual beings who are capable of providing reward and punishment. This is the only "law" which the desperate man will acknowledge—being self-convinced of his abandonment from the physical world.

Thus, superstitious beliefs become the law of the countryman. Even when they will not bow to the power of the city, humans may choose to bow to unseen spiritual power. Indeed, the supernatural power offered through religion is most attractive to the desperate man—who has already decided to forsake the natural world. The offer of spiritual things provides a new path of advancement to those who are altogether dissatisfied with the brokenness of the physical world. So, the desperate man can find within religion a blessed respite and a powerful means to transcend the ills of this world.

Superstitions are also powerful in the sense that they often do not tell people what to do. Rather, superstitions are simply spiritual stories. Individuals who hear spiritual stories around campfires, or who are taught them within their families, are often left to determine the "meaning" of the stories for themselves.

When an individual hears a superstitious story, he may decide to aspire to be like a hero in the tale. Or he may choose to take action to avoid becoming a victim like an unfortunate character in a legend. Either way, superstitious tales leave the power with the listener. The listener decides for himself.

And, in this way, religion is superior to government law. In fact, the desperate man will not listen to the government's laws. He is defiant and does as he desires. But within superstitious tales, the desperate man chooses *for himself* what he wants to believe and what he does not. In this there is hope . . . the desperate man may choose to glean life lessons from religion although he rejects guidance from direct government laws.

Ultimately, superstitions are powerful because they place power within the grasp of each individual. The individual is able to determine how he will choose to apply the spiritual belief to his own life. And this detail makes superstitions better than traditional laws written within the city—because those formal laws are *imposed* upon individuals.

The fact that individuals can determine the extent to which they accept religious tales is apparent in syncretism. **Syncretism** occurs when two or more religions meet and the beliefs of each system blend with one another. This is seen every time a religion meets a new culture. The religion transforms the culture, while the culture transforms how the particular religion is practiced within it.

Why is syncretism important?

Syncretism demonstrates the importance of "individual thinking" in religion. Whereas formal law is altogether unconcerned with the thoughts of individuals, religions and superstitions morph with individuals. In other words, religion is a source of incredible power to individuals. Religion provides the means for any individual to reform his behavior by finding role models within tales.

Thus, the ubiquitous, morphing nature of superstitions provides the necessary means to indirectly govern citizens who are beyond the physical reach of the city's police. By holding superstitious beliefs within a culture, a city ensures all people will generally uphold certain virtues and avoid certain types of behavior.

Furthermore, superstitions provide a positive-negative reinforcement capability in the unpoliced countryside. When citizens believe in spiritual powers, they are governed by the thought that good actions are monitored by spiritual beings—who in turn reward good behavior. Likewise, the superstitious man believes his bad behavior is also monitored by spiritual beings—who punish bad behavior. Thus, the religious man is governed by an internal positive-reinforcement and negative-reinforcement.

Overall, superstitions allow the city to govern the behavior of countryside citizens who are beyond the reach of its police. Therefore, religion becomes the law of the lawless countrymen. And in this, religion is remarkably useful—inspiring citizens to personally adopt certain behaviors and standards of personal conduct.

So, why were all ancient human societies religious?

Answer: Religion is the only effective means to influence the behavior of countryside citizens in the far-off expanses of a city's territories. Frankly, no city has ever existed which is capable of monitoring *all* its citizens. It is not possible. But religion can accomplish what legal systems and police forces cannot.

So, what happened to all the non-superstitious people in the countryside?

The answer is clear. Lacking any unifying beliefs, non-religious people in the countryside would have no connection to the city they supported. In other words, an atheist society in the ancient world would collapse—very quickly.

Moreover, atheism offers no sufficient positive-negative reinforcement for the ancient man. Indeed, why should an atheist work to support the city, when he believes creation itself lacks purpose? However, the superstitious man would work to support the city if he believed it were founded by his god, or if spirits desired him to do so.

So, from all angles, superstitious beliefs are the most useful enhancement of humanity. Apart from superstitious beliefs, there is nothing to unify countrymen in common purpose. This is why all ancient human societies were religious. Those with superstitions carried with those beliefs an indirect, subjectively personal law—which governed their behavior inwardly.

Superstitions are dearly held and beloved, but law is unconcerned and cold. Doubtlessly, those with superstitions are vastly more passionate in the maintenance of their own beliefs than the non-superstitious person is in following the law.

The law punishes without hope of reward. In other words, a human government doesn't send out its police force to reward people for following laws. Human government is concerned only with punishment.

But religious beliefs have an *unlimited* reward system—extending even to "eternity" in the afterlife. The hope presented in religious belief is profound and most attractive. It is no wonder why all ancient human societies gravitated to the power contained within spiritual beliefs. Human laws offer only punishment; but spiritual beliefs offer reward.

> For the desperate man,
> For the country man,
> And for the city man,
> Religion is better than atheism.
> This is why all ancient societies were religious.

11:
Religion as the Source of Abstract Thinking, Imagination, Creativity & Logic

As previously discussed, we explored "imagination" and the ability to remember dreams as characteristics which set humans apart from animals (pages 59-68). It is in our "human" nature to think and wonder—constantly exploring abstract ideas throughout each day.

177

In large, humans exist more within their own minds than they do within the physical world. Most human thought is concerned with exploring things which are not physically present. In other words, whereas animals are wired to interact with the physical reality in which they find themselves at a specific moment; humans primarily concern themselves with the inner movements of their mind irrespective of their physical location.

Indeed, the prominence of the human imagination is the direct result of religion. Religious belief *requires* one to walk by faith, not by physical sight. Therefore, since all ancient human societies were religious, the continual use of imagination among all our ancestors has produced in us an inclination to be altogether driven by our abstract minds.

Does this make sense?

The more religious the person, the more they will be inclined to be driven by their inner thoughts.

The more religious the person, the more they depend on their thoughts for survival.

Therefore, religious thinking makes individuals increasingly more imaginative and creative—encouraging them to change their mental perception of the physical world.

Cool, huh?
. . . walking by faith, not by sight (2 Cor. 5:7)

Throughout human history, your ancestors were superstitious—which required them to use their imaginations. And since the *most superstitious* people were the ones *most likely* to survive in the ancient world (due to their hypervigilance), every generation which survived became more and more religious—in turn making the population of humanity more and more dependent upon its imagination.

Have you ever wondered why humans are prone to having their minds wander?

Throughout each day, a person's mind drifts to many different thoughts beyond their physical circumstances.

In fact, as you read this, you might be thinking about what you will cook for dinner. Or, as you read this sentence, you may be thinking about your schedule next week or your plan for the weekend.

Why?

The reason why your mind drifts is that you are the product of countless human generations which were religious.

Religion taught our ancient ancestors to think about things beyond their physical circumstances. And, in time, those individuals who were the most religious—hence most capable of imagining things beyond their physical circumstances—were the ones who were smart enough to *predict* predator attacks and other dangers.

This is why all humans today have minds which *drift*. Ancient humans without the ability to think abstractly—outside of their physical circumstances—were slowly dwindled by predator attacks and other dangerous factors in their environment.

Thus, religion is a vital component of humanity. It taught ancient humans to think abstractly—beyond their mere physical surroundings. Religion was the only means through which ancient humans survived. This is why all ancient human societies were religious.

Get it?

Another way of putting this . . .

Imagine a group of ancient humans. Let's say the "fastest" humans were the ones who were best capable of hunting. Over time those men who were the fastest would have excelled above their peers who were slower.

In our example, if the fastest men were better suited to catch food, then they would have been able to support more children. So, their families would have grown more than the families of the men who were slower.

And, in turn, when the fastest men had more children than the slower men, this would have further increased the population of fast men (because fast fathers would most likely have fast sons).

In this example, we see how the population of fast men would have continued to grow within the group in each successive generation. As long as being fast continued to be an advantage, those who were fast would continue to grow in population. Over time it is likely the population of the entire group would become "fast," because even among "slow" families, the fastest sons would have excelled more than their slow brothers.

Make sense?

It is an interesting to consider, and if you are looking to ponder this topic further, read about theories for the decline of the Neanderthal man. It is likely a similar situation took place—where the Neanderthal families slowly dwindled due to them being stockier and slower than their counterparts.

So how is this related to "imagination" and religion within ancient humans?

It is very similar. In the ancient world, the clan leaders who told the most inspirational campfire tales would have been more capable of rallying others to follow them. Thus, the populations of the most superstitious grew as they coalesced into strong clans of inspired people. Then, in a further reinforcing fashion, each individual began to use his own imagination more and more—similar to the clan leader who inspired him. Then others would share their own religious tales— further inspiring and encouraging others to grow stronger in their own superstitious beliefs.

And, over time, human societies became increasingly more imaginative and driven by abstract thinking. Indeed, the system itself rewarded strong story-tellers—so people increased in their ability to imagine and think religiously.

Now, when you have an entire group of humans who are each inclined to think in abstract religious terms this provides the framework for the development of other abstract thinking—such as mathematics, logic, philosophy and sciences.

Therefore, religious thought precedes the development of all these things. Apart from religion, there is no ability for other types of abstract thinking to develop in human societies.

I'll repeat . . .

Religion is the pathway to mathematics, logic, philosophy and sciences. Humans had to learn to think religiously before they could think abstractly in other ways.

Why?

Religion is *purely subjective*. Thus, a person can believe in something before they have anything else. No objective proof is required for religion.

In other words, when a myth was told, people believed it without the need for "proof." And, in this subjectivity, religion is incredibly powerful. People can believe in a religion without objective proof. This means religion precedes all other forms of abstract thinking. Religion precedes everything and represents the first step of humanity away from the purely physical thinking of animals.

Humans began to think abstract which were religious and *subjective* first (superstitions, myths, tales, religion). Then, after religion formed this basis of abstract thinking, humans began to think abstractly in things which did require *objective* proof (sciences).

:::*Sidebar for Apologists*:::

Many people fail to understand the purely subjective nature of religion. Religion finds its power in subjectivity. Religion does not require objective proof. Sure, some religions have objective systems—like the Bible in Christianity. And, within the Bible's teaching itself, statements can be made which are objectively true *in that system*. For example, saying God created Earth in the Bible. However, to *believe* what the Bible says is a purely *subjective* choice. In other words, one does not need to "objectively prove" *God created the Earth* in order to "subjectively believe" *God created the Earth*. I can subjectively believe in God's creation—even if I cannot objectively prove it to a skeptic.

This is how apologists mess up. They assume the Bible as a religion must be "objectively proven." But it doesn't.

The Bible, and all religions in fact, are based on subjective faith—encouraging listeners to believe. As such, religion is remarkably powerful and totally independent of the scientific requirement for "objective proof."

Perhaps apologists would be most wise to abandon discussion of religion as something to be objectively proven. Return to the discussion of religious faith in its original form—subjectivity. And by doing so, you can join with ancient religious leaders who encouraged people to "believe," rather than awkwardly attempting to get atheists to concede to cold, "objective proof." Religious leaders for time immemorial inspired people to subjectively adopt beliefs, not cold arguments.

  :::

Religion subjectively explains origins. Religion is capable of subjectively explaining events which put all things in motion within creation; whereas mathematics, logic, philosophy and sciences require the framework religion provides. So, people must be capable of religion before they are capable of any other type of abstract thinking. And, religious human groups are the most inclined to think abstractly—hence provide the framework for other abstract systems of thinking to develop.

  This is remarkable—especially when considering the absurd arguments of atheists against religion. Without religion, there is no such thing as logic. Indeed, all abstract truth requires a tracing back to a non-physical Reality. And, religion provides that framework of Reality—which otherwise would not exist.

In other words, you cannot get non-physical thoughts from the merely physical—as atheistic naturalism supposes.

Let's suppose, as atheists do, that the natural world is *all that exists*. If physical matter is all that exists, then there is no way to evaluate one's own "thoughts." If only physical matter exists, then even the most profound thought of the atheist would be nothing more than a chemical reaction in his brain. And, it is impossible for mere chemical reactions to compare themselves with one another to determine which is superior. Therefore, atheism needs to presuppose the "supernatural." As atheism states its position, it depends on the supernatural presence of logic to evaluate thoughts.

Religion itself is superior to atheism in this regard. Religion is unapologetically subjective—being founded in individual choice and belief. This means those who are religious have no problem accounting for the presence of non-physical things, such as logic. The religious person can merely "believe" logic exists as a part of the created Reality—and it does.

But, in the atheist's faulty position, he cannot explain how non-physical things, such as logic, can arise from merely physical brain chemical reactions. Or, in his attempt to do so, the atheist undermines his naturalistic position. Therefore, he must concede the existence of the supernatural—at least in forming the basis of Reality.

Furthermore, the abstract thinking developed as a result of religion in ancient humanity forms the basis for many aspects of society.

For example, by assigning "supernatural" meaning to coins and paper, humans are able to *represent* large amounts of physical items. So, a piece of paper may represent thousands of cattle, and be traded for them. In this way, the concept of money is connected to the supernatural—as one is required to use his imagination to grasp the value assigned beyond the mere physical form of the coin or piece of paper.

In other words, if paper money were placed before a dog, it would mean nothing. But if paper money is placed before a human, he desires what it *represents* beyond its merely physical form.

Therefore, without supernatural thinking, the concept of money does not exist. And, the principles upon which human societies have always existed—in trade and commerce—cannot exist.

So, why were all ancient human societies religious?

Because apart from religion, there would be no such thing as imagination, mathematics, logic, abstract thinking or monetary trade—all things which were vital to the survival of ancient individuals and their communities.

Neat-o, right, Daddy-o? Made you look.

187

12:
How to Use Myths for Posturing & Protection

I want to make this a playful chapter, because the topic is especially fun. But this is also a very serious matter—if indeed you ever find yourself immersed within a dangerous situation similar to the one I describe below.

The topic . . .

How to use Superstitions and Myths as Weapons

Imagine you find yourself in the midst of an ancient world—where there are no police and no one to rescue you from those who seek to rob you. You do not have an army, and all the groups who live near your group have armies.

Sounds rather bleak, right?

Sounds rather hopeless?

Do I have your attention?

Dwell on that thought first until you feel desperation. Feel what it would be like to be isolated and incapable of protecting those you love.

Once you grasp that feeling of desperation, continue reading . . .

Indeed, if we were to find ourselves in a situation like this, we would be overwhelmed with despair. But we must realize it was this situation which daily afflicted our ancient ancestors.

But, as I will show you, religion can help you in such situations—where you have no other means of recourse. Truly, religion can be an incredible weapon when wielded properly by those who have no other physical options.

However, in my discussion of the gravity of this topic, I must confess: My experiences have gained for me an intolerance of 21st Century atheist snobbery against devout, religious people of the past. Lately, nothing annoys me more than those who ignorantly criticize ancient people—so please excuse my frankness: *If at this point you are inclined to criticize religion or religious people*, set down this book, experience suffering for yourself then return later. Then, perhaps after enduring suffering for yourself, you can gain appreciation for the respite offered by religion to otherwise hopeless people.

But, *if you can already understand and feel for yourself the desperation I am describing*, keep reading and prepare to be further enlightened. As your heart grows additional empathy for your desperate ancestors, you will begin to understand the blessed utility of their superstitions, myths and religious beliefs. If you assess yourself to have such an empathetic heart, continue reading . . .

Returning to the scenario, imagine you are a member of an ancient group of humans. Let's say there are 15 people in your group. You estimate the three rival groups who live just a couple miles from your group each have much larger populations than your group. You believe they may have an alliance with one another—or at least a mutual understanding which prevents them from attacking one another.

I reckon it is irrelevant why your group has been left out of the alliance. Perhaps the generation of humans before you somehow slighted the elders in the other groups. Nonetheless, you are in a desperate situation and the other 14 people in your group are looking to *you* to somehow rescue them from a seemingly imminent attack from the other three groups.

You may be inclined at this time to consider your options. . . .

First, you rule out the possibility of defending yourself militarily against the other groups—being certain you lack the numbers to physically defend your territory if attacked.

Yet, you must safeguard yourself from attack *somehow*. If ever the other groups were to attack you, they would do what was common: Killing your men, raping and enslaving your women, enslaving your children, and plundering your goods and livestock.

So, although you lack the military power to defend yourself, you must find a way to *somehow* safeguard your people.

Ruling out the first option, **second**, you may be inclined to think of offering a trade alliance to the surrounding groups. But, since you lack means to defend yourself, offering a trade alliance to these other groups may serve to *inspire* attack. Indeed, if you and some of your people were to travel to the other groups with crafted goods to trade, what would prevent them from simply robbing you?

Moreover, bringing goods to these groups may give them a heightened awareness of your lands. They may see your crafted goods, and rather than choosing to trade with you, they may choose the much more expedient option of marching to war against you. After all, attacking your group would allow them to get *all* your crafted goods for *free*.

If you are lucky, the surrounding groups may choose to put a garrison of five soldiers in your village, simply to enslave your people as they force them to regularly provide tribute payments to the surrounding groups.

After thoroughly considering the option of offering a trade alliance, you are rightly dissuaded from attempting this. It is likely that offering a trade alliance will result in your group's enslavement and confinement to forced labor in the best possible scenario—which to you is obviously unacceptable.

So, what is your *only* good option?

I recommend a **third** option—where you use a myth to protect your group. This third option will present your group's best chance of survival . . .

Minimal Physical Measures and Myth Protection

#1 Do a Land Survey

When you find yourself in the above described scenario, your best bet is to begin by "knowing your land." You need to know every detail of your land because your survival depends on your ability to conceal yourself within it. In the open you are a sitting duck. But if you find a secluded place to put your village you may have hope to survive long enough to build up your population of fighters to defend yourself.

194

#2 Develop a Defensive Posture for your Village

If you were to be attacked, you would want to funnel enemies to specific points where they could be fired upon by your archers. Moreover, you could use traps in certain locations leading into your village areas—so if you ever were attacked you could dwindle the number of attackers before they reach your defenders.

This may be difficult to accomplish, but if you are attacked militarily this would be your best bet when attempting to fight a numerically superior foe.

But obviously we can see there are problems with taking a purely physical approach to warfare in this scenario—where your group is vastly outnumbered and surrounded. So, although these steps are a good start, you will want to use "supernatural" means to protect your otherwise hopeless group. You will want to use "myths" as a means of psychological, supernatural protection. And, thankfully for you, I will show you how . . .

#3 Develop Myths to Govern your People

Often people may wonder at the occasions in which ancient myths were developed. When considering my discussions on various aspects of religion throughout this entire book, it is apparent myths were used for great purpose within ancient societies. Specifically, in this situation (where your group is surrounded by hostile groups), you will be wise to use "myths" to accomplish certain functions for your people. Let's start with "how you can use myths to govern your people" . . .

First consider this question: As the leader for the group in the above scenario, what morals would *you* want to develop in *your* small group?

Think about it.

Remember, your chief concern is to preserve the lives of your people.

This being the case, I recommend the following: Since your survival depends upon remaining hidden from the larger surrounding groups, you will need to find a way to make all your people conform to certain behavior which will allow your village as a whole to remain hidden. It only takes "one non-conformer" to sabotage your entire village—so your use of myths will need to be thoroughly convincing to gain 100% buy-in from all individuals.

Sure, you could simply "command" your people to stay away from outsiders, but how effective would that be?

In the best case, your people may follow your rule for some time. But, at some point people would neglect or defy your rule—and at that point your people would make your entire village libel to destruction. Therefore, being candidly truthful with your people is not a good long-term solution. Eventually they would rebel against your rule.

So, how could you "convince" people to remain hidden without knowing you are "convincing" them?

Answer: Develop a myth.

Myths are good because they allow you to *indirectly* influence the behavior of your people. Myths—when believed—allow you to "convince" your people to stick to a certain behavior without *directly* telling them to do so.

Get it?

Myths are *indirect* ways of influencing behavior. And they are strikingly powerful at steering community behavior when people sincerely believe in the myth.

For example, in this scenario, you could use a myth of monsters in the forest to indirectly convince your people to remain hidden. The monsters could be described as appearing like normal humans from a distance, but upon drawing closer the monster would eat all people whom it could lure.

The myth would need to be convincing. So, to increase its believability you would need to place props—perhaps "remains" left behind by a traveler who was taken. You would need one or two of your people to tell a story about a monster they saw.

Ultimately, if your myth is successful it would result in your people "convincing themselves" they need to remain hidden from strangers in the woods. Then, once the first generation of your people are convinced, they are sure to teach their children. And, in these following generations—which have no firsthand knowledge of the beginning of the myth, your "monster myth" solidifies as a part of your culture.

Along the way, your people reinforce the myth further. "Confirmation bias" occurs when a person believes something so firmly they begin to see proof of it all around them. Soon after telling the first tales of your myth, some of your people begin telling tales about large footprints they saw in the mud, or growls they heard late at night.

Thus, once a good, believable myth is begun those who believe it become participants in its propagation.

Remember your original purpose in starting the myth—to protect your people. So, although in this case the myth is untrue, its purpose is remarkably ethical. The fabricated myth allows you to *indirectly convince* your people to remain hidden. Apart from the myth your people would face probable enslavement or physical death. In this way the myth provides a means of safety to your people who are not inclined to follow your *direct* rules.

A version of this occurs in M. Night Shyamalan's movie, The Village. Although the myth in that movie was developed for different reasons, it shows how the development of a strong myth can influence cultural behavior.

#4 Myth as a Weapon
At this point your people may be convinced to remain hidden. Now to further remove yourself from danger, you should find a way to deter outsiders from the other groups from venturing near your group's village.

This is how I would consider doing it . . .

Collect bones from animals. (After all, your myth states there are shape-shifting monsters in the woods who eat people. So, it is likely the monsters would also eat animals.)

Identify the most likely routes attacking armies would travel into your forest if they were on their way to assault your village. Along those routes, place bones and anything else you can think of which would support your myth.

Then, get a crazy old citizen who is willing to say they met the monster in the woods near a location leading up to your village. (The crazier, the better.) Have him enter the other group's area appearing distressed with a story stating he is a traveler from a faraway country (not from your group). Any injuries the old man has should be attributed to the actions of the monsters.

If the old man performs his function well, it is likely he will "indirectly convince" many of the other group to remain away from certain areas of the forest (where your people live). If, however an individual chooses at any time to challenge the myth and venture into the forest, he will see your bone props and likely become scared and turn around.

After leaving the other group, the crazy old man could return to your group by another route.

If indeed your myth becomes effective at protecting your people—allowing you to live a safe, secluded life as your group slowly builds its fighting population—then the myth is most helpful.

Indeed, a well-developed myth may prevent warfare altogether, thereby saving countless lives. Therefore, a good, convincing myth may be capable of compelling hostile groups to remain away from you for several generations.

So, as I have shown, myths are truly the best hope for ancient people groups who were otherwise physically hopeless.

Get it?

Thus, even in the case where myths are deliberate falsehoods, they have the ability to safeguard people by influencing their behavior.

So, you must ask yourself if it is more ethical to passively allow people to perish, or to develop a protection myth to ward off danger.

What do you think?

If you were a common citizen, would you rather live under the protection of a myth, or be vulnerable to destruction?

The answer is obvious, and human history shows us the preference of ancient humans for myths. Indeed, those who survived did so under the protection and society-molding capability of superstitions and myths.

Throughout human history, the groups who developed myths were the ones who survived. But the groups who refused to develop myths eventually perished. So, if you want to survive, your best bet is to do likewise: Use myths to your advantage.

If you would like to see an example of this, look no further than <u>Robin Hood</u>. To protect themselves from the numerically superior army, the people in the forest developed stories of ghosts in their woods. This ghost myth deterred outsiders from venturing near them—thereby allowing them to remain secluded as they built up their numbers and trained their people to fight.

So, if ever you find yourself in a similar situation, I advise you to use the same methods of your ancient ancestors: Develop a myth to protect your people.

<u>#5 The Morphing of the Myth</u>

Myths are powerfully capable of morphing over time—providing increasingly relevant help to the people who hold to the superstition.

For example, in the case of the surrounded group who developed a myth of woodland monsters, this group can change details of the myth over time. At first, when the myth began, the group could view the monsters as forces *outside* their camp which keep them contained within. But, over time as the group gradually grows in numbers, it is no longer necessary for the people to remain secluded within the forest. Thus, in subsequent generations the myth may be changed.

Now that your group has numbers which rival those of the surrounding groups, your group now has the ability to fight militarily.

So, how can the myth be modified to support this shift in your group's culture?

Simple. . . . Say this: Your leader and his elite army led an epic quest into the forest and slayed all the monsters. They absorbed the power of the monsters within them—gaining intense berserker strength.

To pass on this supernatural power of the slain monsters, the group's leader must merely conduct a "knighting ceremony" for each warrior he selects to bear this mystical power. This addition to the myth would be incredibly beneficial because it makes your army warriors "feel" supernaturally courageous—as if endowed with mystical power. This means if they were called upon to fight, they would be especially fierce—being convinced by their superstition in their firmly held belief.

203

The "knighting ceremony" could include with it a required period of "wilderness seclusion." A new knight could be required to go into the wilderness alone—perhaps deprived of supplies. And, upon his successful return, the wilderness-hardened warrior would be prepared to receive the full mystical power of the group leader during the "knighting ceremony."

Moreover, during his wilderness seclusion, the new knight may experience "confirmation bias"—suspecting he heard or saw the ghosts of slain monsters in the forest during the long hours of darkness. Thus, upon returning to your group, each new knight may in fact further propagate embellishments to your monster myth—thereby making it increasingly more powerful among your growing group.

Are you starting to see it?

Are you beginning to sense the power contained within supernatural thinking?

Myths transform cultures.

After the addition of the "knighting ceremony," your group's culture could find ways to further reinforce the myth.

For example, the group leader should now be called a "king" and be granted a grand title referring to his valorous action in slaying the monsters. Perhaps your group could have banners which depict the slaying of the monsters.

Finally, if ever your group is challenged in battle, the myth would precede your army. Whereas rival armies may simply *fear* one another; *supernatural fear* is something different altogether. Although a physically strong man can be defeated, a physically strong man who is said to be endowed with the mystical power of monsters would strike terror into the hearts of opponents.

Why?

Because myths deny people a "point of reference." No one has ever seen a woodland monster. Furthermore, no one knows what it means to be "endowed with supernatural power from a monster."

Thus, your myth becomes capable of inspiring *terror* within rival soldiers. If your myth is successful, rival soldiers may even add embellishments to your powerful myth. They may begin to say your soldiers also eat the bodies of soldiers they defeat in battle—being driven by the rage of the monster spirits living within them. Or, they may say your soldiers feed captured enemies to a large monster who still lives deep within their woods.

If you were an ancient soldier, would you be bold enough to fight such an army—who is said to possess the mystical power of monsters, feeding on the corpses of their foes?

Certainly not. Sure, the myths *might not* be true, but would you be willing to gamble *your* life in battle against an army said to possess this mystical power and ferocity?

Most likely, the myth would cause enemies to flee in terror. And, as individual soldiers dispersed from the battlefield, it would inspire a supernatural wave of anxiety and terror among the other troops. Thus, a powerful myth can prevent the horrors of war—thereby saving the lives of countless soldiers who otherwise would have perished.

Need proof?

Look no further than the myths about the Minotaur and the caves and mazes it was said to occupy. Indeed, if a myth is developed properly it can hold rival groups at bay for many generations.

There is reason why all ancient human societies were religious. Supernatural myths, when well-constructed and appropriately embellished, provide vast help to those who believe.

And if you believe enough, your beliefs will indirectly convince your enemies to also "believe"—to their utter detriment. Those ancient human societies with the most convincing myths survived. But those who rejected the use of myths perished over time. Those who believed in myths discovered within themselves a supernatural source of superhuman courage. But those who did not believe in myths were left to fight with the physical frailty of their own hands—an altogether hopeless prospect when matched against those who held within themselves the fire of supernatural courage. Thus, the most superstitious societies survived.

Myths & Posturing

When animals feel threatened, they "posture" their bodies to make themselves appear tougher in an attempt to dissuade an attacker.

For example, when a cat is preparing to fight, it puffs out its fur. This serves multiple purposes. By making its hair stand rigid, a cat makes himself appear bigger to his opponent—which may deter attack altogether.

Rigid hair also gives the cat increased touch sensitivity.

Why is this important?

It gives the cat more time to react to a strike from his opponent because the hair will sense movement even further from his body than if it were laying down.

Although humans may "posture" in some similar ways, like puffing out our chests, we have many other means of posturing that are unique.

My personal favorite act of human posturing is the sound of a shotgun. When a shotgun is cocked it makes a distinct sound which causes everyone to freeze.

But, aside from physical ways humans posture themselves, humans most notably posture themselves using their minds. Humans have complex, abstract minds. And within those minds is found humanity's most striking capability: Imagination. Unlike animals, humans readily deal with abstract thoughts which do not require physical items to be present.

As discussed above, humans use their incredible imaginations in their development of myths and superstitions. So, superstitions and myths are actually a form of human posturing—whereby humans raise their sensitivity to threats and deter would-be attacks.

Cool huh?

And, in terms of effectiveness, myths are vastly more effective than even the sound of a shotgun.

Myths have the ability to stave off attacks for many generations. Myths, if properly used, can make the hearts of enemies melt in fear. Myths can cause enemies to flee. Myths can also impart supernatural, god-like courage to believers.

A sword will ever remain a sword. And a shotgun will always remain a shotgun. But the more one "believes" a myth, the more powerful its effect. So, whereas physical weapons are limited by their physical forms; myths are boundless, being capable of achieving anything—keeping in stride with the boundless mind of the believer. Myths can make people incredibly courageous and powerful . . . with ferocity that rivals weapons.

So, when thinking about toughness, let me put forth the point that *religion is the most effective human means of posturing and protection*. It makes believers "feel" incredibly strong, while deterring enemy attack. To cock a shotgun requires you to be standing close enough to danger for your attacker to hear the shotgun. But the use of myths as weapons do not even require you to step foot onto a battlefield. A powerful myth can win battles before they even begin.

In conclusion, let me remind you of a historical fact: Those humans who were good at telling believable myths *survived*; while those who relied only on physical strength *perished*. This is a simple fact.

Religious humans hold within themselves the ability to muster incredible courage and resolve. Non-religious humans lack this supernatural courage and resolve. This is the key difference—the one thing which sifted out ancient humans as either survivors or those who perished.

Atheism is wrong. It attempts to dissuade humans from the use of their imaginations—the only component of their existence which makes them different from animals. Atheism is a truly fruitless venture—a departure from everything human history teaches us about our past. Humans need spirituality because it is an inherent part of our minds.

This is why all ancient societies were religious.

Section V
Collective Identity & Shared Legends

13:
Storytelling & Campfires— How to have an Interesting Life in the Ancient World

Humans need things to break them out of the mundane. Just like humans today, our ancient ancestors also needed entertainment.

So, what was their entertainment?

Music, feasts and events were some of them. But in order to do many of these things, a clan would have needed certain resources and supplies. For example, to make music, one needs instruments . . . to have feasts one needs food . . . to have events or play sports, one needs certain items depending on what they plan to do.

But what is one community activity which requires *nothing*?

Storytelling.

No matter how poor the clan may be, they could always gather around a campfire to tell stories . . . riveting tales of mystic heroes on epic quests, of creatures with magical, wonderous power which defied common thought. Ancient humans telling tales of renewed hope in the midst of tragedy, visions of Heaven and of the Underworld, conceptualizing good moving behind the veil of this darkened physical world, life springing forth from death, and the hope of ultimate justice to bring an end to the suffering of this world.

Indeed, as we explored earlier, the most prominent feature of humanity is the imagination (see pages 19-93). Humans can remember dreams and even dream while they are awake (pages 21-68). Thus, storytelling emerged as a powerful function of dreamy human imagination.

It is no wonder the most successful ancient societies learned to leverage individual imagination for corporate survival. As ancient humans gathered around campfires, they would share tales—giving language to the visions of their mind. As the inner imaginations of each individual carefully delivered the thoughts of his mind to others, it caused listeners to capture the visions for themselves—making them a part of their own minds.

Thus, these visions have danced atop innumerable campfires throughout human history—inspiring those who participated in these ancient clan gatherings.

And, what tales did ancient humans tell around campfires?

Doubtlessly they were tales of supernatural creatures—gods, goddesses and angels . . . heroes and the avenging of foes . . . those who narrowly escaped harm through mystical, divine power. Human history indicates this is so by the ubiquitous presence of religion throughout *all* of recorded human history. Whenever humans told stories, they mixed elements of the supernatural with the physical world. In other words, storytelling was the means through which the dreams of individuals became *alive* through entire communities.

Surely, the tales told were not of ordinary, merely physical events. Because if the ancient humans desired to hear about mundane, physical things, they could readily return to the harsh conditions which afflicted their daily lives.

Instead, when ancient humans gathered, they did so out of a desire *to be inspired.* And as they heard captivating supernatural tales, their hearts were stirred to adopt the tales for themselves— "adding to" stories as they made them more precious within their own minds.

Ultimately, storytelling was the pathway through which humanity advanced. Those clans who told the best stories—and in effect were the most adept at motivating others in a spirit of community—were the clans which grew. Ancient people doubtlessly travelled to be a part of these most inspirational clans—who had the best stories.

After all, in the ancient world, one either joins with those who are strongest or eventually suffers defeat at their hands.

Storytelling has a mystical way of granting berserker courage and strength to listeners. If you were a clan leader, your best hope in building a strong army would be to develop heroic tales which inspire your common men—making them feel as if they are inheritors of a supernatural power granted by the gods. By developing heart-stirring legends, a clan leader could rally men to follow his lead unswervingly—even in the most difficult circumstances.

And when you build a strong army, others want to become part of it so they can find themselves under its protection, rather than the subject of its violence.

Thus, imagination and good storytelling accelerated the growth of ancient cities. Those clan leaders who told the best tales gathered around themselves men who were ravenously inspired in their military duties. The superstitious zeal of soldiers then inspired more soldiers to join. And around these militaristic clans, cities grew. People travelled to be a part of the city which was born from the supernatural vision and imagination of the adept clan leader.

Then, as a city continued to grow in population and land, the clan leader continued to propagate stories to influence the behavior of citizens—upholding agricultural industry as a godly virtue. And, over time, stories told around simple campfires continued to center ancient people around common purpose and shared communal values. Each citizen was inspired by the tales to continue to do his part for the glory of his city as a part of divine will.

This is why all ancient human societies were religious. In essence, religions are centered upon interesting, inspiring stories, events and sayings. A successful religion imparts to individuals the heart-stirring visions of others—allowing the community to accelerate positive effects among citizens.

After all, if I were to have an inspiring dream, it would only benefit me. But if I choose to share my dream with others, this is where the magic occurs . . .

When I share my vision or dream with another, they can become *equally* inspired.

Why is this significant?

Because ancient campfires became inspirational powerhouses! Not only was each individual benefitting from his own dream, but *every* person in his clan also benefitted.

Get it?

I'll say it another way . . .

If I were living in a clan with twenty people, and if each person told *one* inspirational tale, then by listening I would have the potential to be *twenty-times* more motivated than if I were simply living on my own.

For example, one person might tell a story about a hero who fought a great beast. And from this story I might learn to be more courageous. Then another person might tell a tale about the protection provided by the ghosts of one's ancestors. This might inspire me to care for my elderly parents. Then another person tells a story about how the gods control the cycle of planting and grain harvest. This story might inspire me to work more diligently in my duties as a farmer.

Do you see what is happening?

Do you see how this was valuable to ancient communities?

Storytelling became an *accelerant* for the beneficial behavior of citizens. Storytelling continually inspired citizens to seek self-improvement.

And, even more remarkable, the more fantastical and supernatural the tale, the more powerful the effect.

Why?

Because no tangible "point of reference" exists for superstitious tales. The whole point is that the stories were otherworldly. Thus, stories are not bogged down by physical restriction.

Within the mind of the human, eternity abides. And storytelling allows humans to participate in eternity—even as they live within the clay vessels of their physical bodies. Therefore, supernatural tales impart supernatural power to the heart of the believer—granting him the ability to transcend his natural limits.

A myth is capable of providing unlimited self-refinement. Supernatural stories give individuals the means to completely re-shape their person through the adoption of a new vision. Through "belief," a believer can be born anew—choosing to live a new life separate from the life preceding his belief. And, in this fact, we recognize that faith is absolutely boundless—serving as the vehicle through which the human transcends the physical world. This is why the most remarkable tales produce the most remarkable effects.

Additionally, ancient people recognized their own survival depended on those within their clan. So, whatever inspired clansmen to better fight and support one another would have been accepted by clansmen.

After all, to fight against anything which inspires people to better defend you would be most foolhardy. So, the basic form of religion is targeted at improving chances of individual survival via their clan's improved chances of survival through the indirect molding of individual behavior. Therefore, clans were passionate in holding fast to their own myths—because the survival of individuals within depended on corporate motivation within the clan.

In other words, individual "dissenters" would have been rare in successful ancient groups. Those who gathered around the campfire, shared the vision offered by the speakers. To dissent from the rudimentary shared myths would immediately isolate an individual—to their utter detriment, since the survival of individuals depended on the clans which protected them. So, a dissenting individual would by his dissent lock himself outside of the only structure capable of saving him from abuse from rival clans.

This is why all ancient societies were religious. There was a direct *negative-feedback* built within the storytelling system to discourage dissent from community beliefs.

Also, the more one "believed in" the tale, the more powerful the effect. So, human society itself provided a *positive-feedback* for religious faith. For example, those who actually "believed" there were ghosts in the woods, were the least likely to die in the woods—from predators, hypothermia, bandits, getting lost, injury, and so on. Over time, those who possessed the strongest "belief" in campfire tales were the ones who were the most vigilant, and therefore the most likely to survive long enough to have children. Then, when those superstitious people had children, they would obviously teach them the same beliefs.

Simple.

Over the course of many generations, the population of the most superstitious people increased as those who did not believe became casualties to predators, bandits, injury, hypothermia, et cetera, or dispersed from the city when faced with hardship.

So, why do humans tend to think communally?

Because we are the product of countless generations of storytelling. We are all descendants of people who lived in clans where effective positive- and negative-reinforcement loops continually inspired individuals to fit in with community vision.

A remarkable thing which sets humans apart from animals is that we benefit from the imaginations of others. In fact, we borrow the experiences of others unapologetically.

Need an example?

Humans use language to convey abstract thoughts of things which are not physically present before the listener. So, within human nature we are inclined to listen and believe stories because humanity is communal. By listening to the words of others, we gain a larger situational awareness. Humans dream and remember their dreams, then they share "dreams" with other humans. Thus, humans mold and shape the minds of other humans as each of us learns lessons from one another. In this way, humans benefit from the imaginations of others.

So, why in the world would atheism try to stifle this beautiful process by denying people religion?

Lately, I have pondered the position of 21st Century atheism in relation to the development of humanity. I find when atheists argue against religion, they demonstrate they lack understanding of the purpose of superstitions.

Supernatural beliefs held by clans actually saved the lives of individuals. Religion kept our ancient ancestors faithful to one another despite the many temptations to disperse to their own physical interests.

I find it most bizarre for atheism to deride religion so ruthlessly when religion was the only mechanism through which human life gained a foothold in the ancient world. In other words, without religion, humans would have been left as mere, physically-weak beasts. Religion was the means through which the imagination of humanity developed—enabling him to survive in the midst of a harsh physical world. Without religion, there is no such thing as "abstract thought"—which means ancient humans would have altogether lacked the means to use their imaginations to develop civilization.

Therefore, regardless of whether one desires to be religious or not, the contributions of religion to humanity should be acknowledged. Over countless generations, religion has been a faithful companion to humans in every clime and place. So, to abandon (especially without replacement) such a faithful companion who sustained one's very ancestors would be most foolhardy.

For countless generations humans have survived within their imaginations—constantly thinking of the abstract, spiritual things at move in the world around them. Superstitions actually make life interesting. When living a mundane life, fantastical tales would have added imaginative depth to daily activities.

For example, the ancient farmer, as he stood in his fields, may have begun looking for *goblin* tracks—wondering if they were eating his grain during the evening before retreating to the solace of their holes during the day.

Or the traveler on the road would drift to thoughts of campfire tales. And, in doing so, the traveler's eyes would begin interestingly probing the passing countryside from atop his wagon—ever searching for signs of *werewolves*. It is funny to consider, but such imaginative thoughts—no matter whether they are "objectively true" or not—add flavor to otherwise mundane events.

Yet, in a most bizarre, un-human way, atheists in the 21st Century now beckon others to abandon the liveliness of religion in preference for just living in a dull, physical world.

For me, I much rather prefer to live in a world alive with imagination and religious thinking. Superstitions have always been the spice of human life. Our imaginations are what define us as human. To deny spirituality is indeed foolish—when spirituality is demonstrated to be the premiere tool which allowed human societies to survive.

Those who were superstitious told tales to inspire community—leading others to rally under a common banner. But those people without superstitious tales to bind them together were eventually lost throughout the history of our ancient past. Therefore, superstitious people survived while atheist people did not. This is why all ancient societies were religious.

14:
Trauma Survival & Subjective Belief

In the previous chapter we discussed the importance of campfire storytelling to the development of clans and cities.

When understanding the bleak circumstances in which ancient humans lived, supernatural tales granted them the "will to live."

What do I mean?

Well, let's imagine you are an ancient soldier who has been wounded in battle. If you think on merely "physical things," what motivation do you have to continue to fight? What would compel you to fight further if you have been wounded?

Indeed, an atheist soldier would have no hope of an afterlife to inspire him. Yet, superstitious soldiers are capable of supernatural courage and perseverance.

How?

A soldier who believes he will be rewarded in the afterlife for his valor will fight beyond any temptation to flee. A religious soldier will push himself beyond any physical injury—eager to claim the supernatural prize he believes awaits him.

Need proof?

The ferocity of Norse warriors can be directly attributed to their belief in Valhalla. And, the more a Norse soldier believed in Valhalla, the harder he would fight. After all, if one believes he is a spiritual being who is fighting for divine glory there is nothing which could dissuade him from the accomplishment of his mission. Thus, although an atheist warrior would flee the battlefield to save himself; the Norse warrior—like all those who hold genuine belief in the supernatural—will fight to the point of exhaustion or injury. Then he will continue to fight—being inwardly inspired by his firmly held religious beliefs and his hope of glory in the next life.

Get it?

Once you do, you will readily understand why all ancient human societies were religious. When times are tough, the weak-spirited disperse. Those who do not have religious belief inwardly compelling them to endure eventually run away to save their own skin. But those who are anchored by genuine religious belief within their hearts could not be dissuaded from it—no matter what happens. Therefore, the most religious cities had the fiercest warriors—eventually battering all the faithless cities into absolute obscurity over the countless generations of humanity.

Frankly, without religion humanity cannot survive. History proves this.

Let's use another example . . .

Let's say you are an ancient person who is starving. If your entire life is based on merely physical things, you will lack the mental discipline to press ahead despite your pain. After all, if this physical life is all that matters, what will compel you to continue to fight for your life when everything appears hopeless? And, in these painful moments, as your body continues to pine away,

231

you may have the thought enter your mind which always visits those who suffer: *Death would be better*.

And, once your atheist mind begins to entertain this thought, there is little which could be done to dissuade it. Within an atheist society you would be surrounded by those who are all likewise hopeless—being incapable of seeing anything beyond the present time of physical suffering. When everything is agonizing pain, why indeed should you continue to fight for your life? After all, you had a couple of children who moved away from your present tragedy, so you know your genes will live on.

So, as an ancient atheist, what would compel you to fight for another day?

The answer: Nothing.

Absolutely nothing, in fact.

But, if you happen to be an ancient *religious* person who is in the same situation, you will have within you a supernatural wellspring from which you can continue to draw—no matter how depleted your physical body may become. Thus, for the ancient religious person, perseverance becomes a part of their fabric. Religious people survive. They survive through remembering inspiring tales and firmly fixing their spiritual sight on reward in the afterlife (2 Cor. 5:7).

Got it?

So, what is the result?

Well, as this principle plays out throughout countless human clans and cities over the course of innumerable generations, we see the most superstitious humans are *selected for survival*.

But those who lack genuine religious beliefs are inclined to selfish cowardice when faced with hardship. After all, when an atheist believes in no life beyond this one, and if this life is filled with despair, then there is no true hope to press ahead—especially after an atheist already had children and passed on his genes. However, a genuinely religious person is constantly fed from the wellspring within his heart—refreshing him with inward inspiration and hope to endure all things in faith.

So, what is "genuine" faith?

A person has "genuine faith" when it is shown to stick with them no matter the trial they face. When tested to the uttermost, those who hold fast to their spiritual beliefs are "genuine." They emerge from the fires of this life—refined and pure, resolute, determined and powerful.

233

When we consider how atheists interact with those with genuine faith, this lack of understanding is what causes many problems. I'll explain . . .

French philosopher, Rene Descartes said, "*Cognito ergo sum*"—which means "*I think therefore I am.*"

Whereas a religious person is guided by a particular story or book; atheistic belief is typically traced back to an atheist's acknowledgement of his own consciousness as the highest truth.

Read this a couple times to make sure you get it.

Why is this important?

The atheist position is founded on searching for "proof" for things. First the atheist must start with "proving" himself, then he looks for physical "proof" for things around him. So, ultimately, atheism is a continuing quest for *objective* proof.

But the religious position is superior. Notice above that the religious person is guided only by a story or what is contained in a book. When a religious person is thus guided, the practice of religion is altogether *subjective* and personal.

234

Therefore, atheism deals exclusively with *objective* things—directed at dryly explaining reality; but religion deals with *subjective* things—directed at inspiring people and helping them survive trauma.

Therefore, to mesh together the two different worldviews is like comparing apples and oranges. They are different, and just like apples and oranges, atheism and religion are inwardly governed by different processes: Atheism is concerned with *objective proof*, but religion is superior in being concerned primarily with *subjective*, personal inspiration.

So, why does this matter?

Genuine faith requires no proof.

I'll say it again . . .

Genuine faith requires no objective proof.

This is a major point. Since religious beliefs are designed to help people survive trauma subjectively, then it doesn't matter what on-lookers think about the particular religious beliefs of a survivor. Therefore, in the grandest sense "God's existence" does not need to be "proven." Nor does a believer need to "prove" his beliefs. Sure, he can explain his faith to others. But his choice to believe is purely subjective—and it doesn't matter what others think about his faith.

For example, let's say I am a religious person who survived multiple battles—with my faith helping me to press ahead despite incredible odds stacked against me. After I have survived battles through my now "genuine" faith, will it matter what another person has to say about my faith?

Of course not.

In fact, the *bigger* the hardship through which my beliefs have sustained me, the more resolute I will be in holding fast to my beneficial faith.

I'll take this one step further . . .

The more hardship one endures with his faith, the more "genuine" his faith becomes. Finally, after a person has endured tragedy to the uttermost, his faith becomes altogether "unshakable." In other words, a battle-tested survivor with "genuine" faith would never deny his faith—regardless of what was said to him. His many years of trauma convince him of God's presence, and he knows what it is like to walk in His presence. Thus, the "genuine believer" completely removes himself from objective validation. The powerful "subjectivity" of his faith is altogether sufficient for him—and he will not depart from it, no matter what.

This is the incredible power in subjective belief—when permitted to grow in the midst of unrelenting tragedy. The subjective is much more powerful than the objective. In fact, subjective faith is transcendent—providing the means for the believer to step outside of the physical world as he learns to walk by faith, not by sight (2 Cor. 5:7).

Yet, in a most backwards way, 21st Century atheists ask for objective "proof" for God—a most absurd thing indeed. And, even more confusing, those who are religious feel as if they owe an answer—working diligently to press the subjective framework of faith into something which can be "objectively measured," as if it is something consisting of physical matter.

But it isn't.

When it comes to supernatural beliefs of any kind, "proof" is unnecessary. Either a person "believes" in the story/tale/myth or they do not. And "believing" is a purely "subjective" act which takes place in the mind of the individual. Therefore, supernatural stories *never* need to be proven. Either a person chooses to believe or not.

Period.

In conclusion, those who have endured suffering through faith should not be badgered by those who have not endured that suffering—intent on stripping them of the only beliefs which helped them endure impossible hardship.

And, above all, atheism should never attempt to dissuade people from religion.

Why?

Atheism is an altogether failed system, incapable of producing any enduring ancient city. All ancient human societies were religious. This shows us that human societies prosper *only* when citizens are indirectly guided by subjective religious stories. So, if one were truly concerned for the well-being of his fellow human, he would inspire him to become *more* religious, instead of dissuading him from it.

Yet, atheist humans who were hemmed in with dry objective "proof" as their inward governing force frankly have never produced successful, enduring societies. In fact, atheism has never survived long term. When times get tough, those without superstitious faith crumble.

In other words, history teaches us something quite grand . . .

Without religion, human societies collapse.
Therefore, human societies need religion.

Indeed, due to its purely subjective nature, religion is the best means to foster community among citizens. Religion provides a direct link to the hearts of believers, and it requires no proof or outside validation. And, as more citizens believe in a campfire story, the story becomes even more powerfully capable of promoting positive change in the community. Thus, religion fully benefits from "peer pressure" while maintaining its subjectivity within each individual.

Therefore, an effective religious belief system is beyond refutation by "proof," because those who have "genuine faith" could not be persuaded to depart from their faith (since genuine faith is revealed by perseverance in that faith).

For this reason, proponents of religion should never shy away from the powerfully "subjective" nature of belief. Religion never needs proof. And, in this independence, religion serves as the premiere means to unite people—while paradoxically tailoring itself to each individual's mind through syncretism.

Who cares if a person can "prove" their faith to a skeptic?

What matters is whether or not the person's religious worldview is capable of empowering him—motivating him to remain true when tested to the uttermost.

Sure, "objective truth" can exist within a holy book—just as one could objectively speak to what occurred in various events contained in the Bible or another text. These would be "objective facts" about the religion itself.

For example, saying "God created the Earth" in the Bible. Within the Bible, this statement is "objectively true." But one does not need to "prove" this statement to another person. One is merely left with the decision whether or not they will choose to "subjectively" believe that "God created the Earth."

Make sense?

The point of religion is not for me to force others into my belief—as if I need to debate skeptics on objective points to pummel them into conceding to my religious worldview. This is not what religion is intended to do.

In other words, our ancient ancestors didn't sit around campfires to *objectively investigate* and *analyze* myths. They just told stories in an attempt to inspire one another—so they could somehow muster the strength to survive together in a brutal world. When it comes to religious stories, nothing needs to be "proven"—just listen to the story, welcome it into your heart and allow yourself to be transformed for the better.

Much confusion in the 21st Century would be undone if readers would carefully consider these fundamentals of religion. . . .

Religion is subjective. Religion is not concerned with providing objective proof to the skeptical. And this is precisely why religion has been such a powerful motivating force throughout human history. It provides all the power of relevant subjectivity. It is sustained by positive peer pressure. And it effectively places itself beyond objective reproach from onlookers.

This makes "religion" the perfect means through which one can survive trauma. When trapped in an impossible situation, a person is incapable of "researching or conducting objective validation tests." But, when one is beyond the reach of all other things, it is the powerful inner subjectivity of religion that can sustain him.

Do you desire this power?

Start by believing something rather than nothing.
Abandon your doubts.
Become religious—like your ancestors before you.
Feel the fire within your heart.
Walk by faith, not by sight (2 Cor. 5:7).

15:
Darkness & Dangers in the Nighttime Wilderness

It is significant nearly half of our lives are spent in darkness—every day from sunset to sunrise.

Although you may be removed from this reality through the use of electricity, allow me to immerse you once again within the conditions experienced by ancient humans. . . .

On the Earth, the hours between sunset and sunrise are dark. Darkness varies depending on the amount of light given from the Moon and stars on a particular evening, or the amount of clouds. Some nights

245

it is possible to see in the dark, but during many other evenings it is completely dark—denying humans the ability to see anything.

Already, I am sure, you see where I am going.

When it was dark, ancient humans couldn't see. And since these humans couldn't see, they were left to "imagine" what might be lurking in the darkness.

I am sure we have all experienced this at one point or another. When walking outside in the dark, we are left to "guess" where the walking path begins and ends. Our minds are left to "guess" the location of trees, bushes and other objects.

And, our ability to simply imagine the reality of the physical world around us, although our physical sight grants us no vision, rewards us immediately. If I cannot visualize with my mind the location of a trench, I will fall into it. If I cannot visualize with my mind the location of prickly bushes, I will fall into them.

So, why were all ancient humans religious?

Answer: The darkness of night *requires* supernatural thinking. One-half of all our hours require us to use our "imaginations" to protect ourselves from potential harm.

Ancient humans did not possess night vision. Of course, human vision can adjust to reduced lighting, but even after adjusting human eyes are inadequate in their ability to fully see in the deep darkness of forests. Therefore, the darkness of night compels humans to think in spiritual terms.

Those ancient humans who possessed the ability to vividly imagine were the least likely to fall into trenches when required to move at night. Indeed, having the ability to "imagine" trenches and other obstacles would have granted those humans with a healthy wariness when their physical sight was restricted by darkness.

When considering the many generations of humans who have preceded us, we can understand how the "ability to imagine" would have been a beneficial enhancement for humans. Those who could imagine were more likely to avoid trenches and other dangers. Over the course of hundreds of human generations, those who were the most adept at surviving nights would have been more likely to make it to adulthood and have children of their own.

In other words . . .

Imagination = Less likely to fall in trench

Indeed, those who are more adept at using their imaginations were *selected for survival*. The more vivid one's imagination, the more wary they become of the darkness.

Let's explore a scenario . . .

Imagine there were leopards who lived near an ancient human group. One morning, the human group discovers a deer carcass which is torn and partially eaten.

Now within this group there are two competing stories which arise to explain this carcass discovery. The first tale says the deer was attacked by a wraith which lives within the trees themselves—darting out at incredible speeds to seize its prey. But the second tale says the deer was killed by a large cat similar to a lion.

Here is the question . . .

Which tale is most likely to inspire fear in the other humans? After all, the goal is to keep all the people safe. So, which explanation is more terrifying to an ancient human: (1) an invisible wraith killing with lightning fast impunity from the shadows of the trees, or (2) a large cat?

The answer is obvious. The wraith is far more terrifying (if in fact you believe it exists).

Why?

The answer is simple . . . Whereas a "point of reference" exists for the large cat; there is no "point of reference" for a darting wraith.

Within the human group, some of the people may be familiar with lions—having viewed them from a distance. In fact, their actual observations of lions may dissuade them from fear. They may remember seeing lions lounging during the heat of the day—thereby thinking of the large cat which killed the deer as a giant, lethargic kitty cat. Thus, the "large cat" explanation may altogether lack the ability to produce fear.

But, since no one has ever seen a darting wraith, no comparison exists. There is no "point of reference" for a wraith that darts out from trees. Thus, if the tale of the darting wraith is accepted, those with the most vivid imaginations will develop great fear. This will grant these spiritual-minded humans with a healthy wariness which compels them to remain out of the nighttime forest *at all costs*.

Thus, if one accepts the straightforward, scientific explanation of the "large cat," it is far likelier they may choose to gamble by going into the nighttime forest. But, if one accepts the spiritual explanation of the darting wraith, he is far likelier to remain out of the nighttime forest. And, if one remains out of the nighttime forest 100% of the time, they have a 100% chance of survival from this risk of predator attack.

249

Thus, the ancient human who believes in the "darting wraith" is *selected for survival*. His superstition is incredibly beneficial. His superstition makes him immune to death by leopard. Moreover, it makes him immune to all other types of misfortune which may happen upon him within the nighttime forest—whether bandit attacks, injury, getting lost or hypothermia.

This is significant, and quickly reveals the usefulness of spiritual thinking. Spiritual tales intentionally deny listeners a "point of reference"— evoking fear which increases their likelihood of survival to adulthood so they can have children. Then, the person who "believed" in the darting wraith, teaches his own children about the tale—in turn increasing his own children's likelihood for survival to have children of their own.

Here we establish the remarkable usefulness of superstitions. It is no wonder why all ancient human societies were religious. The above example clearly demonstrates why superstitious people survived as non-superstitious people gradually succumbed to the dangers of the nighttime forests—whether *predators, bandits, injury, getting lost, hypothermia* and so on.

And, if we combine those broad risks above into one, a "darting wraith" myth might provide within itself an intriguing combobulation of *all* those nighttime forest risks. I find this most interesting. . . .

250

The "darting wraith" myth contains within itself the cold of *hypothermia*—emerging from the trees. This belief would dissuade a cold, weary traveler from sitting down and leaning upon a tree—which may in fact speed hypothermia as the tree saps his warmth. Moreover, if a weary traveler lays down next to a tree, his body is no longer generating sufficient heat from its movement—further increasing his risk of hypothermia. So, the thought of the darting wraith may compel believing travelers to remain on the path, rushing to get to town before nightfall. And as they continue to travel, the person's body continues to generate a large amount of body heat—protecting him from getting hypothermia.

The "darting wraith" myth would also make believers wary of humans they meet on the pathways through the forest—thereby insulating the believer from *bandit attacks*. Remember, no "point of reference" exists for a darting wraith. So, a traveler may see a man from a distance, and supposing the man may in fact be the wraith in disguise, he may hide or turn away from him. If in fact the human is a bandit, then in this case the man's superstition compelled a healthy wariness which saved him from confrontation with a bandit.

The "darting wraith" myth would also decrease believers' likelihood of *injury* within the forest by keeping them away from the trees. This means they would not be likely to be injured by falling branches, tripping over roots, or any other type of misfortune. A believer would be more likely to remain on the pathway—thereby avoiding any potential problems encountered from straying off the path.

Those who believe in the "darting wraith" myth would also be less likely to get *lost*—as they may hold a general wariness of the trees as locations where the wraith may emerge. This may inspire them to remain on the path at all costs.

So, you are left to decide . . .

Which explanation is *more helpful*: (1) the "darting wraith" explanation or (2) the "large cat" explanation?

Surely, the darting wraith explanation is more helpful—because it promotes healthy fear and wariness, thereby influencing citizens to remain away from potentially dangerous situations in the nighttime wilderness. In other words, the "darting wraith" believer is more likely to avoid being found in situations where he becomes the prey of a leopard.

Which explanation is the *most accurate description of danger* in the nighttime forest?

This is an interesting question to answer. It is true the "large cat" explanation is scientifically correct in attributing the specific deer carcass to a large cat. But remember, your goal is to save your clansmen from *all risks*—allowing them to live long enough to have children so that your clan can build its population. So, although the "large cat" explanation is completely correct, it is insufficient in its ability to accomplish your true goal— saving your clansmen from *all risks*.

In other words, believing in a "large cat" does little to protect your clansmen from other risks—such as hypothermia, bandit attack, injury, getting lost, etc. So, we see that the "darting wraith" explanation is in fact superior—because it provides a broad-based level of protection against all potential risks to those who sincerely "believe."

Cool, huh?

This above discussion offers a simple example, but it illustrates the power in superstitious, religious, supernatural, spiritual thinking. Superstitions save lives. But straightforward explanations are ineffective in comparison. Scientific explanations are boring and three-dimensional—being confined to only what we can see, touch, taste, smell and hear. But supernatural explanations are the color of this dull world. They allow us to see all things within a boundless dimension—where physical things take different form and inspire real actions. Supernatural explanations excite us; scientific explanations put us to sleep.

Are you afraid of the dark?

Remember, our discussion of REM sleep on pages 33-57. When our brains do not receive sense data—in this case "sight" data—our subconscious minds attempt to "fill the gaps" by feeding us "guesses" as to what may be contained in the darkness. Therefore, it is common for humans to experience anxiety when immersed in darkness—as their subconscious minds work diligently to prepare their conscious minds to react to what may be lurking in the darkness beyond physical sight.

For this reason, we should reason that "fear of darkness" is truly healthy. In fact, to lack such healthy fear would indicate that an individual may be more susceptible to threats if immersed in dangerous situations. "Fear in moments where we should fear" is especially good—indicating that our subconscious minds are capable of adequately warning us of potential danger. Ancient humans without imaginative subconscious minds were far likelier to be taken off guard by predator attack.

The reason why you fear the dark is because you come from a lineage of hundreds of human ancestors who were wary of the darkness. And their fear of darkness was what enabled them to survive long enough to have children of their own. Thus, healthy fear is truly good and beneficial to the one who has it.

What if you don't fear the darkness?

Then you would be wise to take great care to develop your subconscious mind. You can build your spirituality by practicing religion. This would help you to grow in an aspect of "being" which perhaps you have never before experienced.

If ever you are re-immersed within the wilderness or a likewise dangerous situation, let me persuade you to develop some superstitions about the "unknown" darkness around you. By using superstitions, you can actually save the lives of your people. So, let me encourage you to use your entire mind and imagination to your benefit.

"False negatives" & "false positives"

Ancient humans who heard a rustling bush—and promptly imagined a predator was within the bush—protected themselves immediately from attack.

But ancient humans who heard a rustling bush—and were inclined to think it was nothing—were susceptible to predator attacks which occasionally emerged from such rustling bushes.

Therefore, it is better to imagine danger than to think it is nothing. Because, if you imagine danger, you will be quick to protect yourself against it.

If you imagine danger, and it is nothing, then it is no problem. However, if you think it is nothing, but it is a dangerous predator, then you have a major problem!

So, in all cases, it is wise to use our imaginations to our benefit. Superstitious beliefs (no matter how ridiculous) save lives by granting humans healthy fear and wariness. Those who were not scared of the darkness eventually succumbed to dangers within it.

In order for a generational line to survive to the present, all individuals within it needed to survive long enough to have children. This means you are the direct product of people who *all* survived. This means you are genetically inclined toward believing in supernatural things (regardless of what those supernatural things may be). It is a simple fact. Your mind, being formed as the result of hundreds of generations of people who were *superstitious survivors*, constantly draws you to embrace "visions" of the unseen around you.

On a genetic level, every cell of your human body is drawing you toward superstitious thinking. It is a part of your DNA—as evidenced by the fact that all ancient societies were religious.

Thus, humans have been made increasingly superstitious through the threats they survived in each generation. Although no ghost or goblin may have existed (at least I think, haha), holding to ideas of spiritual things makes you increasingly wary. This translates to a higher likelihood of survival from all physical threats.

Therefore, superstitions about darkness = Survival

This is why all ancient societies were religious. Superstitious explanations were better at influencing community behavior—thereby increasing their likelihood of survival in each successive generation. Thus, over time, ancient societies became increasingly religious.

Neat, right?

<u>16</u>:

Weather & Myths

For the last three days, we have been experiencing lightning storms, and a tornado touched down in a nearby town.

I did not intend to write a chapter on weather phenomena. But, as I sit here with my dog, viewing him cowering under my desk—terrified of thunder, I am brought to the realization which afflicted ancient humans.

So, let's talk about weather . . .

It is no wonder ancient humans thought of weather in supernatural terms. After all, when we grow accustomed to certain weather patterns, it makes us wonder why certain days are different than others. And, things which break "natural patterns" would by definition be viewed as "supernatural." Moreover, reflection on these pattern breaks requires "creative thinking"—which itself is also supernatural.

As we discuss elsewhere, creativity is the result of supernatural thought. Abstract thoughts are those which attempt to capture mental pictures of things not present before us. So, to ponder the cause of lightning and thunder requires "creative thinking." To capture the meaning and cause behind storms requires "brain-storming."

And frankly, although true or untrue, the weather myths told by ancient humans were far more fascinating than 21st Century science explanations. Thoughts of "angels bowling" at least gets people to smile; whereas a meteorological explanation puts us to sleep.

Who really cares anyway?

Elsewhere I explore the importance of "relevance" to people. If information is not relevant to a person, frankly they do not care. The meteorological explanation for thunder is pointless for the majority of people. But laughter is always important. Regardless of where we live, we all enjoy laughing. We all enjoy hearing stories. Therefore, mythology (although lacking "objective validation") actually still bears a far greater relevance to humans today than scientific explanations.

Very few people care about the science behind volcanoes, earthquakes, hurricanes, and so on. But if I am good at spinning a tale or telling a funny joke, it would bear "relevance" to most people—allowing them a temporary respite from stress in their lives.

Thus, we discover the ancient world. Ancient humans were afflicted with many dangers and hardships. So, the ability to escape from that dangerous world through imagining the activities of "gods and goddesses," whose actions were mirrored in the environment, was truly relevant and valuable.

Ancient people should not be derided as "ignorant." Rather they should be understood as people going through tough times who found much needed respite in telling tales. Doubtlessly, myths and supernatural tales were sources of inspiration— encouraging people to keep pressing ahead in difficult times. For example, if your mind can capture the thought of God helping you, then you will be moved by an inner strength beyond your own natural abilities.

Faith is incredibly helpful. The more we suffer; the more faith helps. Although we may remain stuck within desperate circumstances, faith persuades us to persevere.

Indeed, if humans today were stripped of their comforts and immersed once again within the dangerous world around them, tales would once again reemerge within human populations. By studying human history, we know this is true because all ancient human societies were religious.

This means there is a cause-effect relationship between a society's ability to tell tales and their likelihood for survival. Yet, human history does not tell us about any successful atheist societies. In other words, none of those atheist societies made it long enough to leave records.

Atheism only works temporarily in a protected world. If humanity is ever again abandoned within the brutalities of an unsheltered world, its survival will depend on the reemergence of human spirituality and imagination. Apart from religion, humanity cannot survive.

So, if ever you find yourself stuck within austere conditions, I encourage you to find respite in supernatural thinking and story-telling. Embrace the proven method of human spirituality. By doing so, your group will find its greatest chance for survival. At night, gather everyone around a campfire—encouraging each other with stories which promote your social values. This is exactly how human societies survived. And this is how your group can survive.

Begin with tales about the weather. Think about where your group needs to go. Then guide them there with your stories.

Section VI
Terminal Reflections

17:
Afterlife: Reward & Punishment

In this book we have been discussing how superstitious beliefs were useful to our ancient ancestors. And, most prominent among all superstitious beliefs are those surrounding the topic of the "afterlife."

Indeed, thoughts of "life after death" are foundational to religious thinking—allowing humans to comfort themselves as they experience loss of family members.

Although I write about the afterlife in detail in my other books, I will not do so here. However, I will explain the usefulness of the afterlife concept.

<u>So, how is the concept of the "afterlife" useful?</u>

First, the afterlife concept provided comfort to survivors.

Rather than remaining within their grief during the loss of a loved one, ancient humans encouraged themselves with thoughts of the vitality of their loved one continuing to exist—perhaps on a different plane of reality.

Truly, this is not that far-fetched. Consider this . . .

When a person sleeps, his body lies motionless. Yet within the motionless form, the mind of the sleeping man races through dreams. In fact, the man continues to act vibrantly within himself even though all observers would say he is "asleep."

Thus, ancient humans simply transferred thoughts of "sleep" to "physical death." Just as humans were certain those who were asleep preserved their mental faculties as evidenced by dreaming, so also ancient humans became convinced "physical death" was a merely outward appearance while the vitality of the person continued to exist in a dream-like reality.

Cool, huh?

Second, the concept of the afterlife is useful because it provides justice.

As ancient humans looked down upon the body of a deceased man, they would reflect upon his previous life. And, in this reflection they would consider if he were "honorable" or "dishonorable."

In this non-verbalized assessment, ancient humans would consider whether or not the man's physical expiration "fit" the ways in which he lived. In other words, if the man were a "good man," did he pass away in a manner which "rewarded" him? Or, if the man were "dishonorable," did his death properly "punish" him for his bad behavior.

Without a doubt, ancient humans viewed cases which caused them grief and cognitive dissonance . . . where "good men" died young or painful deaths; whereas "bad men" died after many years of prosperity. In other words, the righteous at times received what the wicked deserved; and the wicked at times received what the righteous deserved.

So, how was this cognitive dissonance resolved?

Easy . . . the afterlife.

By thinking in terms of "life after death," ancient humans could simply account for disparities in justice. For, in the afterlife, it began to be thought that justice was finally imparted to all . . . whether in the addition of "punishment" to the wicked, or in the addition of "reward" to the righteous.

Then, this religious thought was extended to all society—positing divine forces to mete out justice for all those who were wronged, and even tracking down those who thought they escaped punishment for secret crimes. And, in this, royal officials, leaders and human courts began to be viewed as agents of the divine—measuring judgment for all.

Thus, we see the concept of the afterlife serves as the great equalizer. It solves all cognitive dissonance by putting forth itself as the location where final justice is measured to every individual.

And, in this way, religion became so powerful it continued to affect people even after their physical bodies expired—whether for good or evil. So, within religious beliefs in the afterlife, ancient humans achieved thoughts of total transcendence. They imagined how they could continue to live even after they ceased to live.

Cool paradox, right? (That is why I enjoy religion . . . it flips everything for the benefit of those who believe—allowing us to gain incredible control in situations where there is no control. Religion's treatment of physical death in this regard is most profound—especially in thoughts of the resurrection. Religion amazingly offers a pathway beyond physical death—which is what makes it so attractive.)

<u>Third</u>, the concept of the afterlife is useful because it comforts an individual as he confronts his fate.

This is significant. When an individual viewed the physical expiration of the generations before him, he was beckoned ever closer to the realization of his own fate— one day, just like all generations before him, the ancient man became convinced he too would physically expire.

Now, under this powerful realization, the ancient man had two options: (1) he could allow himself to be crippled by the thought—avoiding it in denial, or, (2) the ancient man could choose to embrace it, somehow finding hope within it.

Without a doubt, ancient humans took the latter approach. They decided to reclaim death from hopelessness. They decided to see physical death as a portal to a new existence on another plane of reality— similar to how a person dreams while they are asleep. And, through religious belief, a person learns to rejoice even when confronted by his own fate. This is the incredible power of religion. And this is why all ancient societies were religious—growing in incredible faith even in the midst of physical death.

Fourth, the concept of the afterlife is useful because it gives an individual control over his fate.

By thinking of the afterlife, ancient humans found the courage to endure the difficult circumstances they often faced in the brutal world. Through imagining a rewarding afterlife, individuals were no longer left to fear their own fate. Rather they could take control of it. In this there is incredible power.

Pharaohs imagined ways of transporting their wealth into the afterlife. Those who suffered fixed their thoughts on ultimate release from the grasp of pain. And, although one was pulled by illness to untimely physical expiration, he could nonetheless declare himself victorious in a grander, eternal sense.

Last, the concept of the afterlife is useful because it breaks the power of death.

With belief in the afterlife one is released from the fear of death. And, in this way, religious belief in the afterlife imparts extreme courage. Such was the inspiration of Norse warriors—who fought as unstoppable berserkers, intent on gaining for themselves the glory of Valhalla.

And within this aspect of afterlife belief, one unlocks the spiritual power which was held by warriors throughout time immemorial. Once a warrior is guided within by this firm belief in afterlife glory, not even the gates of hell can restrain him from his purpose. His religion gains for him the courage to give his physical body to the uttermost—being convinced of the reward he will be granted even after his body is broken.

To many, these things are most mysterious—being far beyond the mind of the merely physical man. But I am doing my best to teach you—to help you to understand.

Frankly, ancient humans were powerful. Within religion and superstition is power . . . incredible power.

But to the 21st Century human—who is a mere sugar- and dopamine-addicted, undisciplined shadow of what he could be—it is near impossible to reckon the power contained within spirituality. The 21st Century human has difficulty "feeling"—having his senses dulled by constant feel-good sensations on demand. And, in a most fell sense, the pleasures of this fallen world have made many incapable of feeling movements of their spirits.

Thus, the 21st Century man is born, wanes and dies—completely oblivious to the spiritual power handed to him from his ancestors. Frankly, it would be most impossible for one to see anything for himself while his senses are controlled by pleasure. Therefore, if one desires to capture for himself the spirituality of his ancestors, the first step would be to step aside from the things of this world which control one's senses. And, in some healthy self-denial, a person's spirit can be beckoned forth from its infancy.

Stepping aside from 21st Century customs, I have chosen to follow in the firm, time-tested paths of our ancient religious ancestors. They were incredibly religious—and their superstitions were the source of their power.

At all times, I will be careful to avoid the paths of 21st Century atheism—set as it is upon shifting and sinking sand. Atheism has no proven track record. It has no ability to sustain humans. Rather, atheism lures humans away from the spirituality which sustained our ancestors. Atheism is intent in depriving humanity of its one characteristic which has enabled its survival through countless generations . . . Religion.

All ancient human societies were religious.
You are human.
Therefore, you should be religious.

Turn away from the dead ends of atheism.
Take the road of self-discipline and self-denial.
Be spiritual.
In this way, you can conquer death.

18:
Eternal Life Occurs when Written

Sure, thoughts occur *within brains*. But thoughts do not *depend* on brains.

Need proof?

Once upon a time, a man named Daniel had a dream about the End Times. Yet, despite his physical brain having long succumbed to the effects of the grave, his dream still exists in written form. In fact, we can read about Daniel's dream in the Bible.

So, the thoughts of humans are strikingly supernatural—being capable of vastly outliving the physical brains in which they were first derived.

Cool, huh?

Therefore, when one ventures to tell you that human dreams and thoughts are only the result of firing physical neurons within his brain, let him be reminded of how dreams can "live on" for millennia—truly independent of human brains.

In fact, if no one read about Daniel's dream, it *would still* exist in written form. Thus, his written dream now exists *totally independent* of any human brain—being penned in ink on paper. In other words, Daniel's dream is no longer dependent on any human brain. Even if no one reads his words, they nevertheless continue to exist—being captured on paper.

When you understand the above, and how writing allows thoughts to transcend physical time and natural barriers—including death itself—it opens your mind to "eternity." Thus, the concept of "eternal life" is not farfetched at all. Even within the physical world around us we see this principle occurring as the work of artists, craftsmen, writers and others endure longer than their natural lives. So, it is quite clear by the rules governing the physical world, that "eternal life" is something achievable by *any* person attempting to reach beyond his own life span.

And, once you get this concept, the spiritual "afterlife" makes sense. After all, if you become a part of the enduring story of religion, then you "live" on through that religion—where your contributions continue to impact others long after you are gone.

For example, if the words of Christ endure forever, and if you trust in those words, then you are *joining in* that eternal endurance. Indeed, we see Christ desired to accomplish this, by grafting in all future believers into His story—praying specifically for all those who would later believe in the gospel of the apostles (John 17:20). And, because His story continues to live, the memory of *all* believers continues to live on through Him. So, it is quite true in our natural world, that those who trust in Christ—although their bodies may physically expire—continue to live on through the enduring story of Christ (John 11:26).

So, let's relate this to the ancient world.

I will show you how ancient humans first achieved "everlasting life." I will persuade you to believe—for it is in your best interest, my dear friend. . . .

279

Imagine you are a person living a simple life in the ancient world. Every year you plant crops and tend your animals. You care for your family—raising your children in the generation after you.

But, as the years pass in a series of planting, harvesting and winters, your mind draws near to an impending reality: Your days may soon come to an end—in the same way the days of your ancestors ended.

To live is desirable, because it is all you know as an ancient human. Death itself is shrouded in mystery—and completely so. When one passes, they are gone from our interaction. We long to embrace them again, but cannot.

So indeed to "conquer death" is one of the most intriguing and intimate prospects—allowing you as an ancient human to perhaps spend one more harvest year with your children. You have so much knowledge within your mind. And, as the years pass, you become more aware of the fact that when you die all your knowledge will die with you.

Unless . . .

As you stand in your field, considering your impending death on a mysterious unknown day, your mind moves to a vision. There is much you must still teach your children about farming, herding and gathering. Many of these skills must be taught during the different seasons of life—and you must wait for each in turn to present the different scenarios and these teachable moments.

For example, it is best to teach your child about wagon wheel repair when the wagon wheel actually needs to be repaired.

And, as your mind considers the different ins-and-outs of your successful living eked out on your farm, you are once again ushered back to the reality—you might not live long enough to teach your child everything he needs to know about wagon repair . . . or anything else for that matter.

Your mind swirls—realizing you might hold within your mind information on which your future descendants absolutely depend for their survival. But your mortality presents an impossible boundary: Once you are gone, you will no longer be available to coach and mentor your family through different problems they will face.

Are you feeling the dilemma?

Are you feeling the anxiety?

Remember, when one generation in the ancient world "just barely" survived, they might have had much anxiety when considering the potential problems which their children would face in their generation.

Now you reflect on the suddenness with which your parents' death occurred. You reflect on the many things which you wanted to ask them—yet never had opportunity.

And, in considering this, your mind turns to your own relationship with your children. . . .

Then, you feel despair. You let out a labored gasp of air, feeling your heart sink with the thought. Fate is a difficult thing to face—and right now you feel as if it is bearing down upon you: Crushing and pressing.

At this point, you could choose to push aside these thoughts—choosing rather to think on positive things.

Many do, in fact.

Sure, this would immediately dispel your despair, but it would do nothing to increase your children's chances of survival in this harsh ancient world.

So, you decide instead to allow "despair" to temporarily abide within you—resolving to follow it to a better decision. And, by courageously taking this bold approach—confronting your own impending death—you become determined to find a way to achieve transcendence beyond your own death. Surely, it seems impossible, but for the sake of your children, you must find a way. You must learn to speak to your children even after you are gone.

Although you *must* pass away, you do not want your children to feel abandoned or regret. At this time your mind approaches a most paradoxical solution to your problem: *You must continue to live even after you die.*

This is a laughable prospect—especially when one considers the finality of death. Once someone dies, they are gone.

But what if that is not the case?

Is there a way you can continue to teach your children after you are physically gone?

Yes.

How?

By writing.

The most straightforward way in which you can "live forever" is by *writing down* your thoughts. You might not live long enough to fix a broken wagon wheel with your son, but you can write a diagram for him. And, even if you were to pass away, your son could read the instructions many years later.

You conclude if you find significant things on which to write—which are sufficiently helpful—then your instructions could develop into a *felt* presence of your mind with your family after you are gone.

So, in the most basic sense, in the ancient world "eternal life" was achieved when one *wrote* down their thoughts. Writing allows a person to reach beyond his own physical limitations—even impacting events thousands of years after his physical death.

When reflecting on written language—it is by definition "supernatural." Writing defies the physical world—even though it is penned with physical ink and physical paper. Writing allows one to read for himself the thoughts of people whom he will never physically meet. Writing allows one to transport himself to far-off place—which he will never physically experience for himself.

And, in doing so, writing is a "supernatural" venture which is boundless in the "physical" world. Writing is a tesseract which barely intersects our physical dimensions through ink on paper—yet the true depth of the thoughts contained therein can transport us as spiritual beings wherever our minds permit.

So, whereas a skeptic may say they think writing is just a *physical* thing; I propose writing in its base form supersedes the physical altogether. It is the basic means through which humans achieve transcendence. It is a thing which is represented in the physical world by ink, yet it is altogether boundless.

If you want to conquer death—write.

And if you want to "live forever," join the story which never ends (John 17:20).

This is why all ancient human societies were religious. The use of written language directly challenges the rules of the physical world. Ancient humans learned that writing had the ability to conquer death itself. And, since a mere "pen and paper" were capable of conquering death itself, it is rational to assume the human mind itself is likewise capable of transcendence. Those who were "dead" continued to speak through their written words—guiding the actions of the generations after them. And, in this, humans continued to hold an intimate connection with all dearly departed loved ones and teachers.

Therefore, all ancient human societies were religious. It was accepted that the life of a human is not restricted to physical forms.

Rather, humans are spiritual beings who live forever.

My dear friend, embrace the spiritual. Do not be imprisoned by the despair and pointlessness of this physical world.

Take the path of religion.
Walk by faith, not by sight (2 Cor. 5:7).
And you will live forever.

Section VII

Worldview Reconciliation

<u>19</u>:
World Complexity, Wisdom & Religion

This will be a fun chapter. It will contain mostly my musings, but I think you will enjoy them. . . .

The world is complicated—no matter the vantage point from which you view it. Even if you look at the smallest creatures, they are each made of many different interworking parts.

Therefore, studying the world puts one in a paradoxical situation—where every topic needs *more* study, consisting of many different parts which are just as complex as another.

Thus, those who attempt to solve problems with their studies are often struck with a paradoxical realization . . .

"The more I learn, the less I know."

I admit I think this often. The world is so beautifully constructed. And, my unquenchable desire drives me to search for patterns in the grand fabric of Creation.

So, the more I learn, I only learn I need to learn more.

Sound confusing?

It is.

Learning is an uphill climb, and those who excel at it must become content in the pursuit—ever realizing true wisdom lies just beyond their grasp.

For those familiar with Marine Corps training at Camp Pendleton, it is like hiking through the hills. The steps drudge on—endlessly it seems. The cold night slows transforms itself to the brilliance of dawn. And with that sunlight, you gain a new perspective on your march— being able to clearly perceive the route ahead.

As you round the series of hill tops, slowly your path forward becomes visible for miles. Your curiosity draws your eyes to trace out your pathway forward— zigzagging back and forth up many more hills . . . each appearing more daunting than the ones preceding it.

And, then—despair.

Your back aches. Your feet rubbed and sticky in your boots . . . yet you continue to pulse yourself forward with each step.

Those hills had many names.

Now I could tell you the names of those hills, and I think you would still like me. But if I told you what Marines would call them, I think you might like me less.

Notwithstanding, for me learning is similar to pulsing my way through those hills. Every time I think I have a hill bested—enthusiastic for the finish line—I only realize I have many more hills to navigate in the heart-bursting maze ahead of me.

Every time I learn something new, my mind is drawn to different topics which are intertwined with the first. Thus, trying to "figure out" anything becomes an overwhelming maze of endless attempts at reconciliation.

293

My eyes continue to dart forward on my future path—tracing out whether my current path successful takes into account each twist and turn in the wilderness surrounding me.

When I write I move to achieve certainty with my reconciliations—ensuring I am not leading myself into a disastrous gulley or ditch. Now I may not have mastery of *all* the wilderness complexity which passes behind me with each pulsing step forward. But I can see *forward* clearly. I can trace out my path with the light of dawn. And I will be faithful to tell you what I see ahead—helping you to join with me as we navigate the wondrously complex trail before us.

There is no finish line . . . only further discovery.

So, why does this matter?

Because "spirituality" puts the journey to discovery in proper perspective. To be a true scholar, one must become at peace with the journey through the mountains. And religion is the most faithful companion in that peaceful, continual journey.

Religion teaches us from the very beginning that we ourselves do not possess all the answers. And this requisite humility is perhaps one of the most necessary traits of a scholar.

In my own life, I note when I pray for wisdom, I find more knowledge and a deeper perspective. My prayers receive answers—yet I never arrive at the achievement of *complete* wisdom. I sense how my prayers for wisdom are used to direct my steps forward—helping me to focus my efforts to find needful answers. Thus, the emphasis is on the journey itself, not the finish line.

But if I did not have religion, then any wisdom I possess would be "my" wisdom. And, by believing I am the source of my own wisdom, my pride would become a rising distraction—causing me to lose sight of my pathway ahead. Thus, religion is most powerful in guiding me to keep stepping forward, while I trust that wisdom will continue to be delivered to me. In other words, religion is powerful because it teaches I do not need to do everything on my own.

Moreover, a scholar who believes he knows everything about a topic will be enticed to offer incomplete conclusions in order to appease his pride. Yet, if a man is tenured by humility, he cares not for how he is esteemed by others. He can be frank and direct—even graciously conceding points to his opponents. This latter man is the one which I venture to become.

And, religion is capable of transforming us into such men—who are tenured by humility, moving forward while dismissing the empty praises offered by others. In fact, religion teaches us to step aside from such distractions which tempt us to look away from the path forward.

When a man becomes religious, he becomes self-disciplined through healthy self-denial. And his religious practices harden him against distractions from his purpose.

In other words, when a religious man breaks the hold of "money" over him, he can no longer be "bought." When a religious man is accustomed to fasting and self-denial—he cannot be enticed by the pleasures of this world, nor distracted from his path forward. And, when this religious man lives for eternal glory, he finds the strength and courage to endure any hardship offered to him by this world.

Thus, the religious man becomes content with each step forward. He finds peace within each painful pulse forward—being certain his pathway is drawing him to a moment of spiritual transcendence. Therefore, this religious man becomes a good teacher—having no earthly incentive, nor a desire to bring glory to his own name. And, such a man possesses great discipline—devoting thousands of hours to study and reflection. Thus, such a spiritual man can be anonymous, seeking only to bring glory to the Name of God.

Nowadays, however, there are many false teachers who desire only to make a great name for themselves—to achieve wealth and the things of the world. And, in their pursuit of worldly gain, they willingly participate in leading others astray. They teach incomplete counsel—instructing others in things they do not understand.

In the 21st Century, these false voices have become so loud, and so promoted, that even when true voices venture to speak forth from the wilderness, the message of wisdom is never heard. The soft voice of true wisdom is seldom perceived amid the competing shouts of false voices—as each peddles frantically to achieve worldly wealth for himself.

More than anything, 21st Century needs a return to *sincere* religion—to let go of pride and worldly pursuits—to establish righteous teachers who will lead people in the good path out of sincerity. Therefore, sincere, self-denying religion can be used to help humanity reestablish true wisdom—separate from the worldly pursuits and agendas of worldly men.

So, what can spirituality teach us about reality?

Reality is exhaustingly complex. Even physical reality is utterly beyond comprehension—let alone spiritual reality. But spirituality is the correct pathway to beginning any fruitful journey to discovery.

Spirituality teaches an individual to be humble and at peace within himself *first*. Thus, the sincere religious person learns to set aside the corrupting desires for money and worldly pleasure. This provides a central position from which the person can venture further in his studies—unbiased and genuinely seeking the well-being of others.

Then, spirituality teaches a person that there is a world beyond their physical abilities to perceive.

Think about it . . .

Is this true?

Absolutely it is!

On a microscopic level there are countless creatures everywhere around us. All around us there are invisible radio waves—each carrying songs from radio and television stations. Even within your own body there are so many different processes taking place which escape your notice.

If you stop and think, there are so many things occurring next to you—and within you—that you will never see for yourself, or even comprehend.

And, considering this physical reality, spirituality is a vastly superior worldview than atheistic naturalism.

Why?

Religion more accurately portrays reality.

Whereas atheistic naturalism tries to teach you to depend on your senses; spirituality tells you from the very beginning that your senses are unreliable—that there is more which exists beyond your physical senses. And in doing so, spirituality better prepares individuals to interact with creation as it exists. A spiritual person can maintain humility—readily accepting there are many things, physical and spiritual, occurring around him which escape his notice.

All around us a world moves beyond our ability to perceive it.

An Empty Room

Let's consider a scenario . . .

Suppose you find yourself in an empty room in an abandoned house. The windows and doors are shut—causing an eerie silence to settle around you.

All of us have been in similar situations before. Perhaps your mind is drawn to occasions where you entered your home in the evening, where you were the only person there. Or perhaps you can think of times where you walked through a parking lot where no other people were present.

In these situations, we might be inclined to say we are "alone." Indeed, our physical senses tell us so. When we look around, we see no one else—so surely, we are alone, right?

But the reality is we are never alone. Even in a physical sense, we are *never* alone.

Why?

Think about it . . .

Within a couple feet of you there are many insects—maybe even burrowing underneath where you sit or stand. And surely those insects—although disregarded as "lesser beings" by humans—are nonetheless just as capable of agency as your pet dog or cat.

And, even more astounding, your body itself consists of countless helpful bacteria and creatures within it—each doing their part to help you digest food and fight off invading parasites. In fact, the microscopic activity within your own body is incredible.

Have you ever used a microscope to observe the behavior of microscopic creatures?

They are just as animated as your family dog. If you observe a microscopic slide you will see creatures who are chasing one another. You will see others which are moving and gobbling up food particles.

Really, these microscopic creatures are no different than any other animal—although they are very small.

So, we see if one declares himself to be "alone"—it is an ignorant dismissal of the *many* physical creatures all around and within his body. Each microscopic creature deserves validation and consideration.

You may ask yourself, "What's the point?"

The point is that spirituality is a far more accurate position than non-spirituality. Ancient humans knew this. They readily acknowledged the existence of spiritual beings beyond their ability to perceive them. This is why all ancient societies were religious.

In all these things we see spirituality is a far more advanced, and accurate, position. So we can rightly say, *"Just because we can't "see" something, doesn't mean it doesn't exist."*

In fact, there is much more about the physical world which escapes our senses than we actually perceive. Therefore, it is a most foolhardy position to oppose spirituality on principle. If humans are drawn to neglect even the components of their own bodies— forgetting the agency of the myriad creatures *within* them—then how could a human be so bold to declare that spiritual things do not exist?

However, you are not alone and spiritual things do exist. The area around us is ever astir with supernatural activity. Thus, we see superstitious people were correct all this time. Whereas a superstitious person would be inclined to feel as if he is being watched in the empty room; the non-superstitious person would wrongly assert his opposition to this thought. But the superstitious person was *always* right in his assertion that he wasn't alone.

Although it might not have been an *invisible goblin* watching the ancient man, he was nonetheless being watched at all times by *something*—whether a spider or a fly. Perhaps it wasn't a ghost who stirred the superstitious person, but the cascading movements of thousands of bacteria within his body. Notwithstanding, in all cases where the superstitious man felt as if he were being watched or acted upon by an agency apart from his mind—he was correct. Thus, religion helps us to derive a more accurate portrayal of the complexities of physical life as well—teaching us that beyond all physical things exist additional layers of mystery. In this way, religion is stunningly more accurate in portraying physical reality than naturalism!

And, this is why all ancient human societies were religious. When the opposing, stifling voice of atheism is silenced, humans intuitively acknowledge the supernatural. Humans intuitively feel the spiritual world around them—being capable of "feeling" beyond their limited physical senses. It is only when humans are deceived otherwise in the abandonment of their imaginations that they declare otherwise.

In conclusion, I encourage you to follow in the footsteps of our religious ancestors . . .

"Believe" in *something* good rather than believing in *nothing.*

Trust your ancestors: Become spiritual.

Section VIII
Warning

20:
Never Trust a Spirit who is Susceptible to Pain

When interacting with supernatural creatures or beings, I am convinced humans should take measures to protect themselves.

Of course, a person who is skeptical of superstitions will dismiss all supernatural stories as mere falsehoods. But this should not rule out the possibility of truth being contained within some superstitions. In other words, even the most skeptical should remain guarded when dealing with supernatural creatures.

In myths and tales, we find there are often supernatural creatures who are "good" and those who are "bad."

Why?

It is interesting to ponder—especially if one believes creation began in a "good" state.

This leads to further questions . . .

How did "evil" begin?

And how could one determine if a supernatural creature were "evil?"

Truly, if an evil supernatural being were to appear to us, we can be certain it would not admit to its own wickedness. More likely, an "evil" supernatural being would attempt to deceive us into thinking it "good." And then, only after manipulating us to its purposes, would the duplicity of the supernatural being come to light.

So, what is the best means to determine the inner motives of a supernatural being?

I offer that any creature who is *susceptible to pain*, will *eventually degrade into seeking after its own interests*.

Make sure you understand this before you choose—if ever—to dabble with spiritual beings. Even the most benevolent spiritual creature, if capable of feeling pain, will eventually sell you out to further its self-interests. This is precisely why ghosts and similar beings should not be trusted. They could start out seeming "good," but as opportunity presents itself eventually the ghost or spiritual being will betray you.

Therefore, if you plan to trust any spiritual being—trust the One who is incapable of suffering harm. In the supernatural world, God is beyond any possibility of being hurt. He is not susceptible to pain, and therefore trustworthy.

So, how is God different?

And why are His angels incapable of evil?

I think these are great questions which strike at the root cause of moral perfection and the original state of humanity.

Although Christ for a time became susceptible to pain during His earthly ministry, He is now incapable of being hurt by anything—being infinitely more powerful than everything in creation. Therefore, God (Father, Son and Holy Spirit) can be fully trusted. After all, God has nothing to gain or lose from us since He already possesses all and is not susceptible to pain. Hence, God is not self-seeking: He would never betray us for selfish purpose, but is truly benevolent.

And, by extension, God's angels are also truly benevolent—being fully aware of God's protection upon them. Since angels are inwardly assured of God's abiding protection, angels have no need to fear pain, nor to protect themselves from harm. Thus, angels are truly benevolent when sent forth as messengers—with no hidden self-seeking motives. Although the Bible speaks of different types of angels, it must be understood the words of a true angel would be altogether trustworthy and reliable—bearing in them no intent to deceive humans.

However, "fallen angels," also known as demons, are different altogether. The Bible explains demons choose to appear to humans as "angels of light" (2 Cor. 11:14). This is done to initially deceive humans into following their counsel. And, doubtlessly humans who are naïve to the hidden purposes of demons choose to follow them willingly due to their magnificent, brilliant outward appearances of benevolence.

Because humans lack experience in the spiritual world, it is possible for demons to trick us. They can appear as just about anything—angels, ghosts, aliens, etc.

But, like I said earlier, any spiritual creature who is susceptible to pain is self-seeking at its core. When creatures are capable of feeling threatened, they will ultimately begin to step on whoever is in their way to provide for themselves.

When we look at the condition of the earth itself, this is the principle which governs all lifeforms as they vie for survival. Sure, within the fallen world there are many symbioses which exist—but when pushed to their uttermost, creatures even abandon symbiosis as they strive to protect themselves. Thus, even in the physical world, a biological symbiont can become a parasite. So, be wary of a supernatural creature who at first appears to be your friend, because it may turn out to be a spiritual parasite.

This is an important principle to understand when seeking to interact with *any* spiritual being. Although for a time a ghost or spirit may desire to form a mutually beneficial symbiosis with a human, eventually the spirit will forsake that partnership in preference for his self-interests.

So, at all times, if you ever decide to dabble in spiritual things, exercise a healthy wariness to guard yourself against the inherent duplicity of spiritual beings.

The Bible tells us that even if an angel were to appear, we should immediately ask him if he serves the Lord Jesus (1 John 4:2).

Why is this important?

An angel who serves the Lord Jesus will not have duplicitous, self-seeking motives, but will be truly benevolent. A true angel of God will not lead us astray.

311

Because a true angel of God is under the full protection of God, the angel feels no threat and is unconcerned with seeking his own well-being. He is inwardly assured of God's protection abiding on him—hence he can exist in moral perfection.

When we understand this principle, it gives us further insight on the human condition. . . .

You may ask yourself how sinful humans can be made morally perfect in Heaven.

When understanding the interaction between pain and sin, it becomes clear: In this fallen world, humans are sinful by nature because inwardly we all feel threatened when pressed by hardship. And, in the most distressing situations, humans are inclined to be self-seeking rather than benevolent in order to save their lives and the lives of their loved ones. Hence, we are sinful by nature— inclined to be self-seeking to the extent we will step on others to provide for our own well-being.

Make sense?

Please make sure you understand.

But originally when humans were created in the presence of God, there were no threats (Gen. 2). Since God was with humans in the Garden of Eden, humans were thereby inwardly convinced of God's abiding protection. Adam and Eve had no need to seek their own self-interests because they were convinced God was providing in all ways for them.

And, in the restoration of all things, humans who are ushered into God's heavenly presence will become inwardly self-assured of God's abiding protection—similar to the angels of God. In the presence of God there is no need for humans to be self-seeking because they "know" inwardly God is providing for all their needs.

Then, in the slow passing of eternity, the emphasis is no longer on "linear" time. Minutes and hours are no longer a concern. Whereas humans in the fallen world were immersed in linear time, needing to survive each moment of time in order to make it to the next; humans in Heaven will have no need to think in terms of survival—and hence no functional purpose for the "counting" of time.

Thus, in Heaven, the concept of time is replaced by an emphasis on "being." Simply "being" in the presence of God and others—experiencing each moment in its fullness will be a distinctive of Heaven.

Of course, this red herring discussion could continue on without limit, so perhaps it is best to end it with an appeal for you to read my other books on these topics. In my other books I discuss how Lucifer fell from Heaven and how humanity fell—both by experiences of "pain" which altered their previously assured minds and immersed them in survival-based, sinful thinking patterns.

On the mount, God told Moses to fix limits for the people to prevent them from being hurt by God's inherently powerful and therefore dangerous presence (Exo. 19:21). Thus, in the Bible we can clearly account for the fall of Lucifer from perfection as a result of him choosing to foolishly venture too near to God's inherently dangerous presence (Isa. 14:13). And in the resulting pain he experienced, Lucifer's original desire to draw near to God was altered in his heart—as he now wrongly viewed God as "causing" the pain. Therefore, the fall of Lucifer and his shift in inner motivation can be accounted for by a proper understanding of the relationship between pain and sin.

In a similar fashion, Adam and Eve fell when subjected to the pain caused by the fruit from the "tree of the knowledge of good and evil" (Gen. 3:7). God warned them to avoid eating from the tree—but they did so to their detriment.

Many plants contain toxic properties—especially things like cardiac glycosides. And that is why we should avoid eating from random trees! So, in other words, there was a reason why God told them not to eat from that tree.

So, if two perfect humans—Adam and Eve—were poisoned, how would they have reacted?

Frankly, they had no "point of reference" to explain why their hearts started to race. There were no books on horticulture to tell them why their chests tightened or why their bodies broke out in feverish sweat. And there were no medical personnel to tell them why their stomachs clenched and pulsed with waves of excruciating pain. Finally, they were left to collapse on the ground beneath them—at the mercy of seemingly unceasing moments of agony, each passing to usher in another.

How indeed would perfect humans perceive such pain?

We can say confidently such a poisoning would change how Adam and Eve viewed the world around them. For the first time they felt pain—and even more troubling they knew they could be hurt, and even killed. Within their minds they began to suspect and blame one another. Then their minds turned to blaming God for putting this tree in the garden in the first place.

After the initial effects subsided, Adam and Eve arose from the ground. Still feeling the lingering effects of the poison, it is likely their intestinal tracts moved quickly to flush themselves of the digesting "fruit."

Have you ever wondered why Adam and Eve chose to clothe themselves?

Pain explains it quite easily.

When a human is hurt, it is instinctive to put pressure on the part of the body which is hurt. Or, in the case of Adam and Eve feeling the extreme intestinal effects, they would have instinctively put pressure on their abdomens—being unsure of what was causing the intense pain within. And, to hold constant pressure on their stomachs, it is natural to think they would have tied vines and leaves like a belt around their waists.

As the pulsing pain of the fruit passed with each round of diarrhea, the leaves of their garment can be easily accounted for. Being unsure why their lower bodies were responding in such painful purging, it was instinctual for them to cover those "private" parts.

Simple.

But I digress. I hope this discussion has been sufficient in demonstrating our point. Any creature—spiritual or physical—who is "susceptible to pain" can be expected to be inherently self-serving. And, this is why you should never trust a spiritual being other than God and His angels.

Be wary of the corruption inherent in all pain-susceptible spiritual beings. It is advised if ever you encounter a spirit, you test it to make sure it's a servant of the Lord Jesus—and hence truly benevolent (1 John 4:2).

Section IX

Conclusion

21:
Dire Conditions

Dear friend,

I have enjoyed our time together. As a fellow traveler, I would like to offer you some final encouragement.

Difficult times happen . . . Tragedies. Trauma.

I have found it is always best to *prepare for the worst and hope for the best*. Although we never desire hard times, we should prepare for them.

So, let me ask you . . .

"Are you prepared?"

Surely, when we are living in abundance, we have friends aplenty—all people remain close in abundant times. But when we descend into a time of suffering— where our goods pine away, we are often forsaken. And, at those times, isolation can make suffering overwhelming.

However, the practice of good religion can provide for you an inward friend to stick near your side in the midst of the most terrible trial. In the book of Daniel, God sent His Angel to protect the men who were cast into the fiery furnace. In the book of Job, God spoke from the storm—giving Job encouragement to prepare him for the next stage of his life.

Likewise, I pray you will be ushered into this most precious aspect of true religion. Religion can grant you a personal relationship with God. And, as you create this blessed partnership with your Creator, you can gain the power to endure tragedy. I urge you to remain true to the path set before you.

Are there hypocrites within religion?

Yes. But why should the actions of "hypocrites" deter you from the good religious path before *you*?

There are many crazy people in the world. And many crazy people are drawn to the warmth and hospitality of the church. In time, the crazy people declare themselves to one of their number. Then, upon being viewed by others, people will set aside religion because they disagree with some of the crazy people who are within and bear lip-service to it.

But you must understand many of the "hypocrites" contained within religion are not truly self-disciplined, self-denying followers of that religion. Bear this in mind and do not let their distractions dissuade you from your own spiritual journey.

Be mindful of people who are within a religion but not wholly adherents of its teachings. Do not let such false people detract you from your own sincere worship in religion. Crazy people will be crazy, but you should not let it affect your own religious practices.

Look rather to the good examples of the faithful within the Good Book. When you are inclined to view an undisciplined hypocrite, look rather to the example of the disciplined prophets and apostles. Set your vision on those good examples as you aspire to take your place at that heavenly gathering. Pay no heed to those who lack self-discipline—other than persuading them to abandon worldliness.

At all costs, avoid the siren call of atheism. It beckons you to leave the sure path of religion which was tread by your ancestors. But ultimately atheism will draw you only to destruction. As a human, you are spiritual. Do not let atheism convince you to abandon your spiritual imagination—leaving you as hopeless as a bird without wings.

Indeed, you will survive by taking the path of your ancestors: Step aside from the false pleasures of this world and take the uphill climb of self-discipline. Choose religion.

In Christ,

Genesis Pilgrim

Terms Referenced

:)

www.ingramcontent.com/pod-product-compliance
Lightning Source LLC
La Vergne TN
LVHW091247080426
835510LV00007B/153